FINANCIAL CRIME AND CRISES IN THE ERA
OF FALSE PROFITS

Keynotes in Criminology and Criminal Justice Series

This Series is design to provide essential knowledge on important contemporary matters of crime, law, and justice to a broad audience of readers including students, educators, researchers, and practitioners alike, and in a format that is not only authoritative, but highly engaging and concise. Nationally and internationally respected scholars share their knowledge and unique insights in comprehensive surveys and penetrating analyses of a variety of major contemporary issues central to the study of criminology, criminal justice, and social justice more generally. Forthcoming and planned Series books cover such areas as electronic crime, race, crime and justice, white-collar and corporate crime, violence in international perspective, gender and crime, gangs, mass incarceration, police and surveillance, financial fraud, and critical criminology.

I invite you to examine the Series and see how these readable, affordable, topical, and highly informative books can be used to help educate a new generation of students in understanding the social realities surrounding crime and justice in both domestic and global perspective.

Henry Pontell, Editor
Keynotes in Criminology and Criminal Justice Series
Distinguished Professor, John Jay College of Criminal Justice, CUNY
Professor Emeritus, University of California, Irvine

FINANCIAL CRIME
AND CRISES
IN THE ERA
OF FALSE PROFITS

Robert H. Tillman
St. John's University

Henry N. Pontell
John Jay College of Criminal Justice

William K. Black
University of Missouri, Kansas City

New York Oxford
OXFORD UNIVERSITY PRESS

Oxford University Press is a department of the University of Oxford. It furthers the University's objective of excellence in research, scholarship, and education by publishing worldwide. Oxford is a registered trademark of Oxford University Press in the UK and certain other countries.

Published in the United States of America by Oxford University Press
198 Madison Avenue, New York, NY 10016, United States of America.

© 2018 by Oxford University Press

Library of Congress Cataloging-in-Publication Data
Names: Tillman, Robert, author. | Pontell, Henry N., 1950- author. | Black, William K. (William Kurt), 1951- author.
Title: Financial crime and crises in the era of false profits / Robert Tillman, St. John's University, Henry N. Pontell, John Jay College of Criminal Justice, William K. Black, University of Missouri, Kansas City.
Description: New York, NY : Oxford University Press, [2018] | Series: Keynotes in criminology and criminal justice series
Identifiers: LCCN 2016051102| ISBN 9780190639198 (pbk.) | ISBN 9780190639204 (ebook)
Subjects: LCSH: Commercial crimes. | Financial crises.
Classification: LCC HV6768 .T547 2018 | DDC 364.16/8--dc23 LC record available at https://lccn.loc.gov/2016051102

9 8 7 6 5 4 3 2 1
Printed by Sheridan, United States of America

TABLE OF CONTENTS

ACKNOWLEDGEMENTS

First, the authors thank all of the reviewers who gave us excellent feedback on the original manuscript: Michael L. Benson, University of Cincinnati; Timothy A. Canova, Nova Southeastern University; Jason Davis, Clayton State University; Mary Dodge, University of Colorado, Denver; Lisa A. Eargle, Francis Marion University; Laura L. Hansen, Western New England University; William C. Heffernan, John Jay College of Criminal Justice, City University of New York; Kristy Holtfreter, Arizona State University; and Dawn L. Rothe, Old Dominion University. Their insights have undoubtedly improved the final product. We also wish to acknowledge the extremely helpful efforts of those at Oxford University Press, especially marketing director Frank Mortimer, who was invaluable in making the *Keynotes in Criminology and Criminal Justice Series* a reality. We are also indebted to our editor, Steve Helba, who has coordinated all publishing details not only with this book, but with all others in the *Series* with incredible ease and professionalism. We also thank the staff at Oxford including Larissa Albright, Holly Haydash, and Patty Donovan for their tireless efforts on our behalf. The late Gil Geis and Steve Rosoff continue to inspire our work. Finally, we thank our families and wives, Loretta, Miho, and June for their love and support.

ABOUT THE AUTHORS

Robert Tillman is Professor of Sociology and Director of the Graduate Program in Criminology and Justice at St. John's University in New York City. He received a Ph.D. in sociology from the University of California, Davis. Dr. Tillman was previously a National Institute of Mental Health Postdoctoral Fellow at the University of Southern California and a Postdoctoral Research Fellow at the California Department of Justice. He is the author and coauthor of numerous articles and books on white-collar crime including *Big Money Crime: Fraud and Politics in the Savings and Loan Crisis* (University of California Press, 1997), which was a finalist for the prestigious C. Wright Mills award and which was awarded the Albert J. Reiss Award for Outstanding Scholarship by the American Sociological Association; *Pump and Dump: The Rancid Rules of the New Economy* (Rutgers University Press, 2005); and *Profit Without Honor: White-Collar Crime and the Looting of America* (Pearson, 2013), now in its sixth edition. In 2016, along with Henry Pontell, he published an opinion piece in the *New York Times*, "Corporate Fraud, Criminal Time."

Henry N. Pontell is Distinguished Professor of Sociology at John Jay College of Criminal Justice of the City University of New York and Emeritus Professor of criminology, law and society and of sociology at the University of California, Irvine. His works span a number of areas including white-collar and corporate crime, criminal deterrence, identity theft, cyber crime, and comparative criminology. He's held visiting and honorary appointments at the Australian National University, Waseda University, the University of Melbourne, the University of Virginia, Macau University of Science and Technology, and the University of Hong Kong, and was a Fulbright Scholar at the University of Macau. He has worked with numerous government agencies including the FBI and the U.S. Secret Service, and has testified before Congress and President Obama's Financial Crisis Inquiry Commission. He is a past Vice-President of the American Society of Criminology, and a past President of the Western Society of Criminology, and is a Fellow of both organizations.

William K. Black is an Associate Professor of Economics and Law at the University of Missouri–Kansas City (UMKC) and the Distinguished Scholar in Residence for Financial Regulation at the University of Minnesota Law School. He is a white-collar criminologist. He was the Executive Director of the Institute for Fraud Prevention from 2005–2007. He was a senior financial regulator instrumental in containing the savings and loan debacle and aiding the successful prosecution of over 1,000 elite white-collar criminals. He is a co-founder of Bank Whistleblowers United.

[1]

INTRODUCTION

"The era of low standards and false profits is over."
(President George W. Bush, 2002)

In the late 1980s the U.S. savings and loan (S&L) industry imploded, with over 1,000 institutions failing, over 1,000 thrift executives and their associates eventually charged with crimes, and taxpayers hit with a $125 billion bill to cover the costs of bailing out the industry. It was, at the time, the largest single financial scandal in world history. In an effort to reform the industry and shore up depositors' confidence, Congress passed the Financial Institutions Reform, Recovery and Enforcement Act of 1989. After signing the act into law, then President George H.W. Bush proudly announced to those assembled in the Rose Garden of the White House: "This legislation will safeguard and stabilize America's financial system and put in place *permanent reforms so these problems will never happen again*" (emphasis added).[1] Thirteen years later, his son President George W. Bush signed the Sarbanes-Oxley Act, one of the toughest pieces of corporate governance legislation in the nation's history, which was a response to the financial crisis in the early 2000s set off by a wave of corporate fraud at many of America's largest companies, including Enron, and Worldcom among other miscreant companies. From the East Room of the White House, President George W. Bush spoke bluntly: "No more easy money for corporate criminals, just hard time.... *The era of low standards and false*

---

[1] Robert Hershey, "Bush Signs Savings Legislation," *New York Times*, August 10, 1989.

profits is over" (emphasis added).² Just six years later in 2008, the country faced a new and potentially much more threatening financial crisis that first emerged in the nonprime mortgage industry but quickly spread to Wall Street where a number of large investment banks either went bankrupt or had to be bailed out by the government. In response to this latest crisis, in 2010 President Barack Obama signed yet another financial reform law, the Dodd-Frank Wall Street Reform and Consumer Protection Act. Referring to his own efforts to get the law passed he remarked: "soon after taking office, I proposed a set of reforms to empower consumers and investors, to bring the shadowy deals that caused this crisis into the light of day, and to *put a stop to taxpayer bailouts once and for all.*"³

Like the smoker in the old joke who says "Quitting smoking is easy... I've done it many times," these examples show that the United States has "solved" the problem of financial fraud and corruption numerous times over the last several decades. But, of course, the fact that the problem continues despite these legislative efforts to stop it only demonstrates that we have not in fact solved the problem, but rather it appears to be getting worse, with waves of financial crime occurring more frequently and with consequences that are more and more of a threat to economic stability.

In his 2002 remarks, President Bush had unwittingly put his finger directly on one key fact. This is indeed the era of "*false profits*"—a time when large firms can make more money through (1) *financial engineering* than they can by improving their products; (2) *gaming markets* rather than being more competitive; and (3) *covering up their failures*, giving the appearance of profitability, rather than riding out the highs and lows of the marketplace. It is an era when even wealthy clients of prestigious Wall Street investment banks like Goldman Sachs can no longer assume that their financial advisors are working for them and not against them; that is, that their advisors are not recommending investments because their firm has bet against them and has structured them so that they are destined to

---

² Elizabeth Bumiller, "Corporate Conduct: Bush Signs Bill Aimed at Fraud in Corporations," *New York Times*, July 31, 2002.

³ "Remarks on Signing the Financial Institutions Reform, Recovery and Enforcement Act of 1989," 25 Weekly Comp. Pres. Doc. 1226 (Aug. 9, 1989) (emphasis added).

fail.[4] It is an era in which Jeff Skilling, the former CEO of Enron, just five years before he was sentenced to twenty-four years in prison for securities fraud, could look into a camera and, without a hint of sarcasm, declare: "We are on the side of angels."[5]

The scope and scale of financial crime is indicated by two analyses in the *New York Times* that show the deep and consistent involvement of major financial institutions in illegal activities. In a 2011 review of SEC actions, the newspaper found that since 1996, nineteen of the largest Wall St. firms had been accused of securities fraud a total of fifty-one times. All of these firms committed further violations despite having promised the SEC not to break the law following their initial violations.[6] A later article showed that as of October 2013, JP Morgan Chase, one of the largest investment banks in the world with 2012 profits of $21 billion, was the subject of seven major investigations into illegal activities, including one involving the bank's role in the subprime crisis that led to an agreement with the U.S. Department of Justice to pay a record $13 billion to settle those charges.[7]

It seems clear that despite a spate of new major laws designed to curb major financial crime by legitimate firms, the problem continues to persist and at ever-larger levels. While many other books have examined individual financial scandals, this book will consider broader questions: (1) how is financial crime linked to financial crises and why do both seem to be occurring more frequently; (2) what essential forms of financial fraud are inherent to modern economies, with variants occurring over and over again in different places around the world; and (3) why has so little been done both to punish those responsible for financial frauds and to address the systemic sources of these white-collar crimes? These are big issues and it would be impossible for a short book to deal with them in a

---

[4] For a detailed discussion of the Goldman Sachs cases, see Staff of the U.S. Senate, Committee on Homeland Security and Governmental Affairs, Permanent Subcomm. on Investigations. *Wall Street and the Financial Crisis: Anatomy of a Financial Collapse* (2011).

[5] *Smartest Guys in the Room*, directed by Alex Gibney (2005, Magnolia), DVD.

[6] Edward Wyatt, "Promises Made and Remade, by Firms in S.E.C. Fraud Cases," *New York Times*, November 7, 2011.

[7] "Tracking the JP Morgan Investigations," *New York Times*, October 22, 2013.

fully comprehensive way. Our goal instead, will be to provide readers with a criminological context for understanding these diverse sets of financial crimes, a way to see what links them together, and a way to appreciate their underlying common forms and sources, as well as the similarities of the responses they provoke. Despite their apparent differences, these events are not unique, nor are they aberrations (as many economists would have us believe), but instead they are rather normal and routine features of contemporary economic life. Such a perspective allows us to see financial crime and crisis in more structured terms and to avoid the more common approach of confronting each fresh financial scandal and financial crisis anew. While the media fixates on the colorful lifestyles of "rogue" white-collar criminals, such as Bernie Madoff, the systemic roots of their crimes are ignored, leading policymakers to formulate "permanent solutions" again and again.

We start by addressing a fundamental question: Why are we witnessing more and more financial crimes, occurring with unprecedented frequency and with consequences that are much more devastating, in terms of the number of people they impact and the damages they inflict, than ever before? Before laying out our broad answer to this question, we consider two possible alternative explanations: (1) people are simply less honest, and more willing to cheat, than they once were, and (2) the increase in financial crime is an illusion created by a sensationalist media.

EXPLAINING FINANCIAL CRIME

A Culture of Dishonesty?

As an explanation for increased financial crime, the possibility that people are less honest than they once were holds some appeal. It's not hard to see evidence of deceit and malfeasance everywhere one looks—from teachers altering students' test scores to professional athletes taking banned performance-enhancing drugs to corporate executives falsifying their firms' financial statements. One popular version of this explanation holds that the United States is in the grip of a "cheating culture" in which "cheating is everywhere" and people of all backgrounds are "breaking the rules to get ahead academically, professionally, or financially."[8] According to the originator of this idea, David Callahan, this cultural trend has resulted from rising social inequality, economic insecurity, a failure of society to punish transgressors (particularly the wealthy), and "America's highly individualistic culture—which glorifies wealth, status, and personal gratification...."[9]

The problem with this argument is that it does not align well with the empirical evidence. It is difficult to find data that directly measures honesty, but there are a number of trend studies that document changes in people's perception of honesty among others. For several decades pollsters at the Gallup organization have conducted surveys in which they ask respondents to rate various professions in terms of their honesty and integrity on a scale that goes from very low to very high. Contrary to what some persons believe, over the last thirty-five years most of those professions have seen their honesty ratings *improve* or at least not decline significantly. For example, in 1976, 15% of those surveyed rated the honesty and ethical standards of advertising practitioners "very low"; in 2012 that proportion had dropped to 6%. For building contractors, 18% of respondents in 1976 and 22% in 2012 rated their honesty as "high." In both periods relatively few respondents rated "business executives" "high" or "very high" on business and ethical standards, but the proportion that did remained about the same at 20% in 1976 and 21% in 2012.[10]

A second, indirect measure of honesty in society is the crime rate. Many dishonest people are never accused of, or commit, crimes, but if levels of honesty had fallen significantly, one might expect to see it in increasing crime rates. In fact, over the last twenty years crime rates have shown unprecedented declines. According to the Federal Bureau of Investigation (FBI), between 1992 and 2012, rates of violent crime plunged by nearly 50% and property crime rates decreased by over 40%.[11]

---

[8] David Callahan, *The Cheating Culture* (New York: Mariner Books, 2004), 14.

[9] "About CheatingCulture," Cheatingculture.com/about.

[10] Gallup. "Honesty/Ethics in Professions," www.gallup.com/poll/1654/Honesty-Ethics-Professions.aspx#1

[11] FBI, Uniform Crime Reporting Statistics —UCR Data Online. "Estimated crime in United States—Total," www.ucrdatatool.gov/.

Financial Crime: An Illusion?

A more radical explanation for the apparent increase in financial crime is that it hasn't happened at all, and that the presumed epidemic of corporate criminality is a hoax perpetrated by a sensationalist media and liberal politicians. This view finds its fullest expression in alternative narratives about the causes of the financial crisis that began in 2008 and was clearly articulated in an op-ed piece in the *Wall Street Journal*.

> A persistent media-liberal lament . . . is that too few financiers have been prosecuted for the financial crisis. But maybe that's because when the Obama Administration tries to prosecute a specific individual for a specific crime, it turns out there was no crime.[12]

The culprits behind the crisis, according to this view, are not on Wall Street but in Washington where government bureaucrats created a housing bubble with policies that encouraged people to buy homes when they could not afford them.[13]

The problem with this argument is that it is contradicted by a massive amount of real data about the role of fraud in the financial crisis. As early as 2004 the FBI was warning about the emerging "epidemic" of fraud in the subprime mortgage industry, noting that "80% of all reported fraud losses involved collaboration or collusion by industry insiders." In a particularly prescient prediction, an assistant director at the FBI warned, "If fraudulent practices become systemic within the mortgage industry and mortgage fraud is allowed to become unrestrained, it will ultimately place financial institutions at risk and have adverse effects on the stock market."[14] The pervasiveness of fraud in the nonprime mortgage industry was indicated in two analyses.

---

[12] "Where are the Criminals?" *Wall Street Journal*, November 27, 2012.

[13] See also Peter Wallison, *Hidden in Plain Sight: What Really Caused the Financial Crisis* (New York: Encounter Books, 2015).

[14] *Mortgage Fraud and Its Impact on Mortgage Lenders*, House Financial Services, Subcomm. on Housing and Community Opportunity, 108th Cong. 6 (2004) (statement of Chris Swecker, Assistant Director, Criminal Investigative Division, Federal Bureau of Investigation).

Based on a review of three million mortgage loans, the consulting firm Base-Point Analytics conservatively estimated that losses due to fraud were over $3 billion annually.[15] Fitch Ratings analyzed a sample of forty-five subprime loans that had been securitized and sold in packages of residential mortgage-backed securities and found that "there was the appearance of fraud or misrepresentation in almost every file."[16] Studies like these led the national Financial Crisis Inquiry Commission (FCIC) to describe the context of the financial crisis as one of a "rising incidence of mortgage fraud, which flourished in an environment of collapsing lending standards and lax regulation" and to conclude that "a crisis of this magnitude cannot be the work of a few bad actors" but rather was systemic in origin.[17]

The argument that it was Washington and not Wall Street that was responsible for the financial crisis bears a striking resemblance to the arguments offered some twenty years earlier by what has been called the "fraud minimalists" in the aftermath of the S&L crisis.[18] The essence of this argument greatly diminishes the role of fraud by thrift insiders in that crisis and instead portrays thrift owners as honest, if sometimes naïve and reckless "gamblers," victims of economic circumstances and bad government policies. In this narrative:

> Honest thrift owners who desperately gambled to save their institutions and failed in doing so, along with moral hazard created by a combination of faulty regulation and deposit insurance comprise, [are] to a large degree, the official record of the savings and loan debacle.[19]

---

[15] BasePoint White Paper, "New Early Payment Default-Links to Fraud and Impact on Mortgage Lenders and Investment Banks" (2007), 2.

[16] FitchRatings, "The Impact of Poor Underwriting Practices and Fraud in Subprime RMBS Performance" (2007), www.fitchratings.com/.

[17] Financial Crisis Inquiry Commission, *Financial Crisis Inquiry Report* (Washington, DC: U.S. Government Printing Office, 2011), xxii–xxiii.

[18] See William Black, *The Best Way to Rob a Bank Is to Own One* (Austin: University of Texas Press, 2014).

[19] Henry Pontell, "Control Fraud, Gambling for Resurrection, and Moral Hazard: Accounting for White-Collar Crime in the Savings and Loan Crisis." *The Journal of Socio-Economics* 34(6) (2005): 756–770.

Once again, the facts do not support this position. A 1989 analysis by the General Accounting Office of the twenty-six most costly thrift failures found evidence of fraud and insider abuse at every one of them.[20] A later study of 686 failed thrifts found allegations of serious criminal fraud (where losses exceeded $100,000) at 66% of those institutions.[21]

If people are not more dishonest than they once were, and the increase in financial crime is real, then how do we explain it? The analysis that follows focuses on systemic, institutional factors rather than on individuals and their characteristics. The argument holds that over the past several decades those institutions that control the flow of money around the world have changed significantly, affecting the opportunities for crime and corruption. The increasing complexity of the global financial system has provided innumerable ways to fudge, fiddle, fix, hide, distort, and manipulate the intricate machinery that lies behind that system. While a full description of the broad changes that have impacted financial markets in the last several decades is beyond the scope of this book, we begin by summarizing some of those changes, specifically, those that have increased the opportunities for fraud and malfeasance.

Our focus in this book is on financial crime viewed in the context of recurrent financial crises. We are aware that these issues raise larger questions about the nature of capitalism, particularly some of its more destructive consequences, as well as the increasing inequality that plagues many nations. These are important topics, but here too, a short book like this one cannot do justice to these complex subjects and the reader is better served by referring to recent works that explore these broader connections in depth.[22] The present book has a narrower objective: it is intended to introduce the reader to contemporary forms of financial crime and to demonstrate how they are linked through their common origins in the socioeconomic process of financialization.

---

[20] U.S. General Accounting Office. *Thrift Failures: Costly Failures Resulted From Regulatory Violations and Unsafe Practices* (Report to Congress) (GAO/AFMD-89-62) (Washington, DC: 1989).

[21] Robert Tillman and Henry Pontell, "Organizations and Fraud in the Savings and Loan Industry." *Social Forces* 73(4) (1995): 1439–1463.

[22] See, e.g., Gregg Barak, *Theft of a Nation: Wall Street Looting and Federal Regulatory Colluding* (New York: Rowman and Littlefield, 2012), and David Harvey, *The Enigma of Capital* (New York: Oxford University Press, 2010).

FINANCIALIZATION

Over the last several decades, the corporate landscape, and the financial services industry in particular, has been transformed by a number of trends. Among the most important, at least for this discussion, has been what sociologists and economists refer to as "financialization": "a pattern of accumulation in which profits accrue primarily through financial channels rather than through trade and commodity production."[23] The broad scope of financialization is captured well in the following passage from journalist Rana Foroohar's book, *Makers and Takers*, where she writes:

> The financialization of America includes everything from the growth in size and scope of finance and financial activity in our economy to the rise of debt-fueled speculation over productive lending, to the ascendency of shareholder value as a model of corporate governance, to the proliferation of risky, selfish thinking in both our private and public sectors, to the increasing political power of financiers and the CEOs they enrich, to the way in which a "market knows best" ideology remains the status quo, even after it caused the worst financial crisis in seventy-five years.[24]

In essence, this trend leads to an economy that is based more on moving money around than on making tangible products.[25] It has had a number of significant consequences, including the following: (1) the financial services industry has come to dominate the economy to an unprecedented extent; (2) many economies, both regional and national, have become increasingly dependent on financial services, which can skew policies in favor of those industries; (3) firms within and outside the financial services industry have

---

[23] Greta Krippner, "The Financialization of the American Economy." *Socio-Economic Review* 3 (2005): 178.

[24] Rana Foroohar, *Makers and Takers* (New York: Crown, 2016), 6.

[25] Former Secretary of Treasury, John Snow told the FCIC, "I think we overdid finance versus the real economy and got it a little lopsided as a result." Financial Crisis Inquiry Commission, *Report*, 66.

shifted their focus from improving the quality of their products or services to increasing the value of their stock; and (4) levels of compensation in the financial services industry have dramatically increased, creating opportunities for individuals to amass large fortunes in relatively short periods of time.

The Growth of the Financial Services Industry

By the end of the twentieth century the U.S. economy had become so dominated by finance that economist/columnist Paul Krugman referred to it as "the monster that ate the world economy."[26] Where profits in U.S. financial industries comprised less than 10% of all domestic corporate profits in the early 1980s, by the mid-2000s that proportion had jumped to over 40%.[27] Viewed historically, wages paid by financial services companies have grown dramatically. Throughout the 1950s, the average wages paid in the industry were about the same as the average compensation earned in all industries, but by 2007 it had reached 181%.[28] This financial dominance has occurred despite the fact that the number of Americans employed in the financial services industry has not actually increased that much in the last several decades.[29]

Thus, the dominance of the financial services sector is found in its scope of activities and not simply in the number of persons employed in the industry. In 1970, an average of 12 million shares were traded on the New York Stock Exchange. By 2000, that number had increased to just over 1 billion shares. The proportion of Americans who owned stock either directly or through mutual funds or pension plans increased from 10% in 1970 to 48% in 2000.[30] This growth in the securities market was tremendously beneficial to Wall Street banks. By 2008, JP Morgan's assets totaled $2.2 trillion; up from $667 billion in 1999. At Goldman Sachs, assets grew from $250 billion in 1999 to $1.1 trillion in 2007.[31] It was this tremendous

[26] Paul Krugman, "Making Banking Boring," *New York Times*, April 10, 2009.

[27] Simon Johnson, "The Quiet Coup," *The Atlantic*, May 2009, 49.

[28] *Ibid.*

[29] Krippner, "The Financialization of the American Economy," 178.

[30] Kevin Phillips. *Wealth and Democracy* (New York: Broadway Books, 2002), 140.

[31] Financial Crisis Inquiry Commission, *Report*, 65.

growth that led to the emergence of "too big to fail" institutions—banks that were so large that the government was forced to bail them out to protect the economy—that gained a chokehold on the economy.

Economic Dependence on Financial Services

One of the consequences of the growing dominance of the financial services industry is that many countries and cities are now highly dependent on finance to support their economies. Global financial centers like New York and London are good examples. Even after the financial crisis of 2008, taxes from Wall Street firms made up 14% of New York State's total tax revenues in 2011. Before the crisis that proportion was as high as 20%. Data from New York City show that in 2010 jobs in the securities industry accounted for 23.5% of all wages paid in the private sector, despite making up only 5.3% of all private sector jobs in the city.[32] In Britain and London this dependence is even greater. In 2007, financial services accounted for 8.3% of the UK's GDP and 18% of London's GDP.[33] In 2015, financial services contributed 11% of all tax revenues paid in the U.K.[34] This dependence has led politicians in both of these jurisdictions to be very protective of financial services industries and to vigorously resist reform efforts and to oppose crackdowns on illegal practices within those industries.

Dependence on financial industries has also occurred because those industries and their business models have begun to permeate more sectors of the economy. As sociologist Gerald Davis observes:

> "Wall Street" is now everywhere, as gas station proprietors speculate in oil futures to hedge their business against shocks in the Middle East, American homeowners find their

---

[32] New York State Comptroller's Office, "Wall Street Bonuses Declined in 2011." News release, February 12, 2012, www.osc.state.ny.us/press/releases/feb12/022912.htm.

[33] Duncan McKenzie, "Economic Contribution of UK Financial Services 2009." *ISFL Research,* 2009, *www. TheCityUK.com.*

[34] City of London Corporation, "Total Tax Contribution of UK Financial Services Eighth Edition" (London: City of London, 2015).

mortgages owned by Norwegian villagers and Midwestern
toll roads end up being owned by Australian pension
funds.[35]

The movement of finance into traditionally non-financial areas is well-
illustrated in a fascinating series of articles published in the summer of
2013 by the *New York Times* which describe how Wall Street investment
banks like Goldman Sachs and Morgan Stanley have begun buying up
companies that store and move commodities—oil, wheat, cotton, coffee,
and aluminum—which gives them the ability to alter the markets for
those goods, and in turn, make huge profits, In a case study, the *Times*
describes how Goldman Sachs was able to drive up the price of aluminum by intentionally delaying shipments of the metal out of a warehouse
it owns, making aluminum more expensive and increasing its profits, but
ultimately costing consumers an additional $5 billion in a three-year pe-
riod.[36] In Chapter 2 we will see how investment banks have also moved
into the markets for electricity and natural gas where they have made millions by similarly gaming the markets for those commodities. In 2014,
Senator Carl Levin, commenting on hearings held by his committee on
investment banks' involvement in commodities markets said: "If you like
what Wall Street did for the housing market, you'll love what Wall Street
is doing for commodities."[37]

But it's not just investment banks that are moving into the "real" (i.e.,
non-financial) economy. Private equity firms, companies that combine
capital from individuals and pension funds to make investments, have
been taking over and privatizing services that were once provided by
cities and towns to their citizens. Firms like K.K.R. and Blackstone have
been buying up ambulance services and fire departments and operating

---

[35] Gerald Davis, *Managed by the Markets: How Finance Re-Shaped America* (New York:
Oxford University Press, 2009), 102.

[36] David Kocieniewski, "A Shuffle of Aluminum, but to Banks, Pure Gold," *New York Times*,
July 20, 2013.

[37] *Wall Street Bank Involvement with Physical Commodities*. Senate Comm. on Homeland Security and Governmental Affairs, Permanent Subcomm. on Investigations, 113th Cong.
(2014), 2.

them as for-profit businesses utilizing a strategy that has worked for them in other areas: "a mix of cost cuts, price increases and litigation." Users of their services find themselves treated not as citizens who have a right to these services, but as customers who are billed for being transported to a hospital or having a fire extinguished. In one case, a homeowner saw his house burn down after the local, privately owned fire services provider took an hour to respond to his call for help and later found himself facing a $15,000 bill from the owners of the company.[38]

Financial Engineering

Just as financial firms have moved into non-financial industries so, too, have many non-financial firms begun to mimic financial services companies by shifting toward an emphasis on financial engineering, with the bottom line represented by the firm's share price. Instead of investing in research, product development, and increased efficiency, many large firms now spend millions of dollars a year, employing armies of lawyers and accountants in an effort to reduce their tax exposure. Reduced tax liabilities lead directly to more favorable balance sheets and higher stock prices. At the same time, a number of large non-financial companies have moved into financial services, providing many services that once were only offered by retail banks, a trend that Olivier Godechot refers to as *bankarization*.[39] A notable example is the retailing giant, Wal-Mart, which offers its customers a full array of banking and money services, from check cashing to money transfers.

The shift toward an emphasis on stock prices by publicly held firms was seen by many observers as a positive trend, one that represented an "investor revolution" in which shareholders would gain a larger share of profits as well as greater control of the firm's operations. Part of this trend was an effort to more closely align executives' interests with

[38] Caniel Ivory, Ben Protess and Kitty Bennett, "When You Dial 911 and Wall St. Answers," *New York Times*, June 26, 2016.

[39] Olivier Godechot, "Financialization Is Marketization!," *Max Planck Sciences Po Center on Coping with Instability in Market Societies* (Paris, 2015), 4.

those of stockholders by making executive compensation increasingly dependent on share prices through the use of stock options and stock awards. Simply put, executives would do well only as long as shareholders did well.

But there is a negative side to these trends. As we shall discuss in detail in Chapter 3, these stock-based compensation schemes gave executives strong incentives to cheat, in particular, to engage in financial statement fraud, to artificially increase revenues or to hide liabilities in an effort to improve the perception of their company's performance and the firm's share price. At their worst, these tactics constituted "pump and dump" schemes in which executives, working with accountants, lawyers, and bankers, conspired to "pump up" the firm's performance measures with false data, reap the rewards of the higher stock prices, and then "dump" their shares before the market caught on to their schemes and the prices plummeted. With these accounting tricks, corporate managers and executives were able to betray investors, not share profits with them.

Big Money

There was a time not too long ago when working on Wall Street or being employed as a trader in the Chicago Mercantile Exchange was a guarantee of a comfortable if not opulent middle-class lifestyle. That began to change in the 1970s as compensation for individuals in the financial services industry began to soar. One way to look at the increase in salaries in the industry is to compare them to those in another profession: engineering. Economists Thomas Philippon and Ariell Rashef estimated that until the 1980s, highly educated finance workers and engineers were paid roughly equivalent amounts. But since that time, the average salaries of financial workers zoomed ahead of those of engineers so that by 2005 financial workers were earning 35% more than similarly educated engineers. This difference in wages is even more pronounced among the top earners in finance, who, by 2005, were earning 250% more than their counterparts in other private-sector industries. In the tristate area (New York-Connecticut-New Jersey) they earned three times as much. Philippon and Rashef also found that in 1980, finance executives were paid on average ten times more than top government regulators, but by 2005 were earning sixty times more.[40] This massive discrepancy may go a long way toward explaining the revolving door between Washington and Wall Street, and the inability of the government to effectively reign in major financial crime.

One might ask what all this has to with white-collar crime? Simply put, with more money flowing through the financial sector, the rewards for illegal activity and the ability of chief executive officers (CEOs) to create perverse incentives through bonuses have grown exponentially. In the 1980s people were shocked to learn that infamous junk-bond king and convicted insider trader Michael Milken was paid $550 million for one year's work by his employer Drexel-Burnham-Lambert. In 2011 dollars that would be $1.07 billion per year, but it would be far less than today's top hedge-fund executives receive, some of whom earn well over $4 billion a year.[41] In these environments the potential payoffs from illegal activity to even relatively low-level employees can be huge, and they are hard for many to resist. Many financial workers come to see that simply changing a few numbers or obtaining insider information about the health of companies can bring them tremendous rewards. For those higher up the corporate pyramid it may be tempting to devise strategies in which their subordinates actually carry out these deviant activities and are more vulnerable to prosecution if things go wrong.

FINANCIAL CRIME AND FINANCIAL CRISES

The above factors have greatly increased the opportunities and the motives for engaging in financial crime, as large sectors within advanced capitalist economies operate like casinos where powerful players are gambling with other people's money. Long before the current financial crisis, Maurice Allais, Nobel Prize-winning economist, argued that financialization had transformed many economies into giant casinos.

---

[40] Thomas Philippon and Ariell Rashef, "Wages and Human Capital in the U.S. Finance Industry." *Quarterly Journal of Economics* 127(4) (2012): 1551–1609.

[41] James Stewart, "In a New Era of Insider Trading, It's Risk vs. Reward Squared," *New York Times*, December 12, 2012.

> With speculation on the currency market, speculation in
> stocks, and speculation in derivative instruments, the world
> has become a vast casino, with gambling tables located at
> all latitudes and longitudes. The gambling and bidding, in
> which millions of players participate, never stops.[42]

Thirty years ago a *Business Week* magazine article warned that we had become a "casino society . . . a nation obsessively devoted to high stakes financial maneuvering as a shortcut to wealth" and cautioned that "innovation and deregulation have tilted the axis of the financial system away from investment and toward speculation."[43] The purveyors of junk bonds and real estate investment trusts promised oversized profits while downplaying the risks inherent to these exotic financial instruments.

But what this model fails to capture is the fact that while in casinos the odds of winning are known and the same for everyone who decides to gamble, financial markets, increasingly, are operating as "rigged casinos" in which the big players are engaged in the equivalent of adding weights to roulette wheels or marking cards at blackjack tables. This brings to mind a quote from the infamous American gangster Al Capone, who was known for his willingness to bet on just about anything, but refused to buy stock. Responding to a reporter's questions about the stock market after the crash of 1929, Capone reportedly said: "It's a racket. These stock market guys are crooked."[44]

Casino economies promote strategies with short-term horizons and immediate payoffs, but whose long-term effects can be very destructive. As Kitty Calavita and her colleagues have described:

> Finance capitalism spawns vast new opportunities for
> fraud . . . perpetrators of financial fraud in the casino

[42] Maurice Allais, "The Worldwide Crisis Today." *Executive Intelligence Review* 26(14) (1999): 11.

[43] Anthony Bianco, "Playing With Fire: As Speculation Replaces Investment, Our Economic Future is at Stake," *Business Week*, September 16, 1985, 78.

[44] "Stock Market 'Too Crooked' for Capone," *Chicago Tribune*, November 3, 1929.

economy have little to lose. The effects of their crimes on the health of the casino or even its survival is unimportant to these financial highfliers.[45]

During the 1980s, for example, savings and loan CEOs orchestrated accounting fraud schemes that guaranteed the ability to report record, but fictional, profits by making massive amounts of bad loans that ensured that their institutions would fail and undermined the integrity of the entire banking system. Similarly, conditions in the housing market of the early 2000s prompted a number of major players in the mortgage industry to adopt the same strategies in making home loans. The firm that seemed to embody everything that was wrong about the industry was Countrywide Financial. Looking back on Countrywide's spectacular rise and fall, a former vice president wrote that the company's "new system of loans and Refis (refinancing loans) awarded to anyone with a pulse, was, in retrospect, long-term madness driven by short-term profit."[46] These destructive, fraud strategies that generate huge, fictional, short-term profits by making bad loans are one of the reasons why casino economies are inherently unstable.

Theoretical and empirical work by economists, sociologists, and criminologists have shown that financial crime is both a cause and consequence of financial instability, an inherent feature of both economic booms and busts. The same conditions that create financial bubbles often create the opportunities for widespread fraud and corruption and those fraudulent practices, in turn, cause the bubbles to expand and ultimately burst. William Black argues, for example, that accounting fraud "hyper-inflates and extends the life of financial bubbles, which causes extreme financial crises."[47] Black explains how, initially, accounting fraud will cluster in a

---

[45] Kitty Calavita, Henry Pontell and Robert Tillman, *Big Money Crime* (Berkeley: University of California Press, 1997), 64-65.

[46] Adam Michaelson, *The Foreclosure of America: The Inside Story of the Rise and Fall of Countrywide, Home Loans, the Mortgage Crisis, and the Default of the American Dream* (New York: Berkley Books, 2009).

[47] William K. Black, "Epidemics of 'Control Fraud' Lead to Recurrent, Intensifying Bubbles and Crises," Social Science Research Network, 2010, 1, http://ssrn.com/abstract=1590447.

certain industry but inevitably spreads as CEOs in other industries will learn that they must match the (false) performance reported by cheating executives in order to maximize their compensation. The result is an "epidemic" of accounting fraud, as was observed in the early 2000s. These epidemics further distort investors' understandings of the performance of corporations and their value, and leads to inflated stock prices which ultimately plunge when their true value is realized. Black's observations are grounded in a larger theory about the causes of executive looting.

In a groundbreaking 1993 article, George Akerlof, Nobel Prize-winning economist, and his colleague Paul Romer argued that certain conditions provide incentives for executives to loot their own companies, engaging in what they called "bankruptcy for profit" or, more simply, "looting." Similar to Calavita et al.'s argument about savings and loan owners' focus on illegally obtained short-term profits at the expense of their institution's survival, Akerlof and Romer's theory holds that, generally: "Once owners have decided that they can extract more from a firm by maximizing their present take, any action that allows them to do so will be attractive-even if it causes a large reduction in the true economic net worth of the firm."[48] Moreover, the total financial losses from looting in one industry may far exceed the illicit profits gained by corporate looters as: "Looting can spread symbiotically to other markets, bringing to life a whole economic under-world with perverse incentives."[49] To illustrate, Akerlof and Romer describe how looting by S&L owners in the Dallas area in the 1980s led to artificially created distortions in the real estate market, leading honest developers to continue building homes, even though the markets were saturated, under the assumption that rising prices would continue into the future. This action exacerbated an existing real estate bubble that soon burst, resulting in a severe downturn in the local economy.

The increasing frequency with which financial crises occur has caused many economic analysts to rethink their views on how capitalist

---

[48] George Akerlof and Paul Romer, "The Economic Underworld of Bankruptcy for Profit," *Brookings Papers on Economic Activity* 24(2) (1993): 2.
[49] *Ibid.*, 3.

economies work. Until recently, the prevailing view, promoted by neo-liberal, Chicago School economists under the banner of what is known as the "efficient market hypothesis," held that an inherent feature of modern capitalist economies is a tendency toward stability. Whenever flaws or contradictions emerge, the "invisible hand" of the market will correct for them. By the end of the twentieth century the efficient market theory had become so dominant among prominent economists that it had attained near religious status as a doctrine, one in which "financial markets . . . play a role similar to that of other deities in guiding behavior."[50]

Yet, despite its widespread acceptance, this view has been challenged by a number of well-known economists who argue that "in the history of modern capitalism, crises are the norm, not the exception."[51] Nouriel Roubini and Stephen Mihm have argued that financial crises are not "black swans," unpredictable and unstoppable catastrophic events, but are rather "white swans," "commonplace and relatively easy to foresee and to comprehend."[52] Roubini and Mimh's views were echoed by the FCIC in its assessment of the causes of the crisis:

> The crisis was the result of human action and inaction, not of Mother Nature or computer models gone haywire. The captains of finance and the public stewards of our financial system ignored warnings and failed to question, understand, and manage evolving risks within a system essential to the well-being of the American public. . . . To paraphrase Shakespeare, the fault lies not in the stars, but in us.[53]

Roubini and Mimh's work is located within an economics intellectual tradition that focuses on "crisis" versus "stability," which often puts them at odds with mainstream economic thinking.

[50] Davis, *Managed by the Markets*, 243.

[51] Nouriel Roubini and Stephen Minh, *Crisis Economics: A Crash Course in the Future of Finance* (New York: Penguin, 2011), 15.

[52] *Ibid.*, 7.

[53] Financial Crisis Inquiry Commission, *Report*, xvii.

One of the more prominent figures in this intellectual tradition is the late Hyman Minsky, who proposed what came to be known as the financial instability hypothesis, a central tenet of which can be summarized as "success breeds excess breeds failure." In times of economic prosperity, financial institutions take on more and more risk—banks, for example, make more loans to finance speculative ventures—ignoring the lessons of previous financial crises.[54] These trends lead to a "euphoric economy" in which "businessmen and bankers" show a "disregard [for] the possibility of failure."[55] Lending practices by bankers and other lenders reflect a cyclical process in which they progress from relatively conservative financing strategies to riskier "Ponzi-financing" strategies which are "often associated with fringe or fraudulent financial practices" (emphasis added),[56] which produce instability in financial markets, which in turn can lead to financial crises and recession. Accompanying these reckless business practices, euphoric economies also often experience reduced oversight by regulatory bodies—what Minsky referred to as "thwarting systems" because they tend to thwart the tendency toward economic instability.[57] With the onset of the financial crisis, Minsky's ideas, which had long been relegated to the backwaters of economic thinking, suddenly enjoyed a renaissance, with commentators declaring the time to be a "Minsky Moment" in which governments are required to step in to right an out-of-control economy.[58]

Economists (with notable exceptions like Akerlof and Romer), while drawing our attention to the larger macro-economic issues, have not spent much time relating them to white-collar crime. Criminologists have attempted to make this link explicit often by employing the concepts of "criminogenic industries" or "criminogenic markets," whose

---

[54] Hyman Minsky, *Stabilizing an Unstable Economy* (New York: McGraw-Hill, 2008), 236–237.

[55] *Ibid.*, 237.

[56] *Ibid.*, 231.

[57] Piero Ferri and Hyman, "Market Processes and Thwarting Systems," Working Paper No. 64 (New York: Jerome Levy Institute, 1991).

[58] John Cassidy, "The Minsky Moment," *The New Yorker*, February 4, 2008.

structure and essential features enable and encourage fraudulent tactics and transactions. Henry Pontell has stated that financial bubbles give rise to epidemics of financial crime that are "neither random nor irrational; they occur when a 'criminogenic environment' creates perverse incentives to act unlawfully."[59] One of the best examples is seen in the nonprime mortgage industry of the early 2000s. There, deregulation and desupervision coupled with modern bonus compensation made it easy for CEOs to create powerful, perverse incentives for employees and agents to make millions of terrible loans likely to default. To aid these frauds and make the loans appear safe, lenders and their agents made millions of "liar's" loans they knew would produce vast numbers of fraudulent statements on mortgage applications and ultimately lead to massive waves of foreclosures.

It is a myth that when lenders sold mortgage loans to investment banks to be securitized, they no longer had any incentive to guarantee that borrowers could in fact pay off those loans. Mortgages could only be sold to the secondary market through "representations and warranties" that the loans were underwritten properly. The endemic fraud in nonprime mortgage origination meant that these reps and warranties were fraudulent and also meant that the originator was on the hook for the losses. The key is that the bank officers were not on the hook for the losses–and they got to keep their bonuses for making fraudulent loans.

Similarly, Tillman and Indergaard (2005) have argued that the New Economy industries of the late 1990s—exemplified by the dot-com industry—were operating within criminogenic institutional frameworks in which, "many of the same figures that orchestrated frauds also worked with political allies to orchestrate deregulatory policies that figured a great deal in the rise of criminogenic conditions."[60] In effect, they were making the rules while they were breaking the rules.

---

[59] "The Impact of the Financial Crisis—Miami," 2010, Financial Crisis Inquiry Commission (testimony of Henry N. Pontell, University of California, Irvine).

[60] Robert Tillman and Michael Indergaard, "Corporate Corruption in the New Economy," in *International Handbook of White-Collar and Corporate Crime*, eds. Henry Pontell and Gilbert Geis (New York: Springer, 2006), 481.

FINANCIAL CRIME: CULTURAL SUPPORT FROM A COUNTERNARRATIVE

We end this chapter by addressing a fundamental question: Why do people continue to engage in these illegal and harmful behaviors despite widespread condemnation in the media, by government officials, and by ordinary citizens (as evidenced by opinion polls where respondents are overwhelming critical of corporate criminals)? The question is similar to one raised by two sociologists, David Matza and Gresham Sykes, who were studying urban, juvenile delinquents in the 1950s. Contrary to dominant criminological thinking of the time, the delinquents they spoke to did not seem to adhere to the values of an alternative, oppositional culture but largely accepted the norms and values of the larger culture, including norms regarding the unacceptability of delinquent behavior. How then did they overcome this apparent contradiction? Part of the answer, according to Matza and Sykes, is that in their behavior the delinquents were expressing adherence to a *subterranean set of values* which stressed the importance of adventure, thrills, and easy money, and which coexists along with the larger culture which presents a different set of values.[61]

Similarly, the individuals who engage in the illegal behaviors described in the chapters that follow do not appear to be part of a criminal underworld, nor do they appear to have been indoctrinated into the values of a deviant subculture, but instead they appear to be relatively ordinary citizens whose values by and large mirror those of larger society. In the ethical narrative presented by the larger culture, acts of financial crime are broadly condemned; popular movies overwhelmingly depict corporate criminals as evil threats to society, news reports vilify swindlers like Bernie Madoff, and corporate greed is routinely denounced by church leaders.

But there also exists a narrative that runs counter to the one expressed in the larger culture. This counternarrative, which is often generated by neo-liberal economists, intellectuals at conservative think tanks, and

---

[61] David Matza and Gresham Sykes, "Juvenile Delinquency and Subterranean Values," *American Sociological Review* 26(5) (1961): 712-719.

right-wing pundits, draws on traditional, libertarian themes that reso-
nate with the distinctly American values of individualism, self-reliance,
and anti-government populism. Here one can find the view that insider
trading, far from being harmful to investors, actually has many positive
benefits including *preventing* fraud by providing quicker information to
investors on the real price of stocks and weeding out small investors who
should not be dabbling in the stock market in the first place.[62] Here one
can learn that tax evasion in the form of hiding assets in offshore accounts
is not a bad thing but is actually part of a process of "tax competition"
that ultimately makes governments more efficient, creates jobs, and
raises standards of living.[63] It is in this narrative that one can discover
that market manipulation by energy traders, as described in Chapter 2,
was actually a "rational response" to a poorly designed system and over-
regulation.[64] It is also here where one finds out that individuals, like the
executives at Enron, who engage in corporate fraud are actually "innova-
tors" who make positive contributions to the overall development of the
economy; as Nobel Prize-winning economist Gary Becker said of Enron
after its crash: "Enron's actions, while self-serving, were generally good for
the economy as a whole."[65] And it is in this narrative that one can discover
that anti-money laundering laws are unnecessary violations of citizens'
privacy rights and futile attempts to restrict the free flow of capital that
can actually harm the world's poor.[66]

[62] See Henry Manne, *Insider Trading and the Stock Market* (New York: Free Press, 1966);
Doug Bandow, "It's Time to Legalize Insider Trading," *Forbes,* January 20, 2011, www.
forbes.com/2011/01/20/legalize-insider-trading-economics-opinions-contributors-
doug-bandow.html.

[63] Richard Rahn, "In Defense of Tax Havens," *Wall Street Journal,* March 18, 2009; Chris
Edwards and Daniel Mitchell, *Global Tax Revolution* (Washington, DC: Cato Institute,
2008).

[64] Robert H. Tillman and Michael L. Indergaard, *Pump and Dump* (New Brunswick, NJ:
Rutgers University Press, 2005) 62.

[65] Gary Becker, "Enron Was Mostly Right About One thing: Deregulation," *Business Week,*
March 18, 2002, 26.

[66] *"Know Your Customer" Rules: Privacy in the Hands of Federal Regulators,* House Comm.
on the Judiciary, Subcomm. on Commercial and Administrative Law, 106th Cong.
(2000) (prepared statement of Senator Ron Paul); Daniel Mitchell, "World Bank Study
Shows How Anti-Money Laundering Rules Hurt the Poor," *Forbes,* April 20, 2012.

These narratives provide a *subterranean* set of values for the men and women who have the opportunities to engage in financial crime, values which serve to rationalize their actions and render them reasonable and legitimate. Financial workers are exposed to these alternate values through workplace seminars, the business press, and the business schools they attend. These values are often woven into the organizational cultures (described in Chapter 5) that create environments that are conducive to corrupt and illegal behavior. These values often lie behind the seemingly callous and amoral comments and conversations of financial workers that suggest, at best, an indifference to the moral implications of their actions.

To summarize, the thesis of this book is fairly straightforward. The increasing financialization of the economy, in the United States and elsewhere, has heightened the *criminogenic tendencies* of a number of industries, particularly the financial service industries. Firms within these industries and individuals within those firms can quite easily feel the pressure to pursue profits through illicit means rather than through innovation or increased competition. These criminogenic tendencies are both a symptom and a cause of financial instability which in turn leads to recurrent financial crises that threaten the economy. The individuals who actually carry out the day-to-day practices through which these illegal goals are accomplished find support and legitimacy for their actions in counternarratives that turn conventional moral interpretations on their heads, and in which these actions are not only seen as nondeviant but as beneficial to society. It is through these processes that epidemics of white-collar crime are connected to financial crises. The next four chapters will describe fundamental forms of financial crime. The goal will not be to provide a comprehensive catalogue of the most important financial crimes but, rather, to describe illegal practices that illustrate the criminogenic tendencies of financialized economies. In each chapter we present a diverse set of individual case studies which, despite their differences in form and context, illustrate the common pressures to pursue illicit profits among the relatively few who control most of the world's money.

THE PRICE IS (NOT) RIGHT; BID RIGGING IN FREE MARKETS

"The methods and techniques of manipulation are limited only by the ingenuity of man."
(Cargill, Inc. v. Hardin, 452 F.2d 1154, 1163 (8th Cir. 1971)

According to most economists, the world's financial markets work because of Adam's Smith's famous "invisible hand": the collective contributions of millions of individual participants form a natural system of checks and balances that determines things like prices and interest rates that keeps the financial system in natural balance. Competition among participants creates a "market discipline" that ensures that no one has an unfair advantage. But is this idealized version of the economy true? What if, instead, certain market participants were allowed to game the system to work to their advantage—as Smith famously warned? This is what appears to have happened in a number of cases in which market participants discovered that even small alterations in little-known price/rate indexes could result in tremendous profits. Because transactions in these markets tend to be zero-sum games, huge profits for some means huge losses for others, and the losers are often people who are not professional insiders but investors, consumers, and municipal bond issuers who assume that the indexes are truly objective measures and that the game is being played on a level playing field.

In this chapter we examine four cases of price/rate rigging to show how theory deviates from reality: (1) the misreporting of natural gas prices to indexes in the early 2000s; (2) recent allegations that subsidiaries of investment banks manipulated electricity prices in complex financial schemes; (3) in what may be the most costly corporate scandal of all times, the deliberate rigging of the London Interbank Offered Rate (or Libor); and (4) the manipulation of foreign exchange (FX) rates by investment bank traders. All these measures are used to set standards for a diverse array of transactions involving a wide range of financial instruments including derivatives so that the number of victims and the losses from these schemes are very large.

These are complex cases, dealing with the mostly hidden machinery of the financial system that remains opaque to most of us and which is accessible only to select groups of workers in the financial industry. But as we shall see, the actions of these small groups and organizations can have an enormous impact on consumers around the world. In what follows, we will sketch out the essential elements of these illicit schemes, describe their similarities and consequences for markets, and link them to broader trends in the financial services industry. These complicated schemes involved extremely arcane financial and technical terms and mechanisms involving numerous details that need not be discussed in order to understand the major underlying components of these frauds. Instead, we will examine the essentials of these illegal market strategies.

NATURAL GAS PRICES

The scandal that swirled around Enron Corporation in the early 2000s brought attention to the ways corporations could game the securities markets by falsely reporting their companies' performance in annual reports. But in the course of multiple investigations into Enron's misconduct, investigators stumbled upon evidence of a related form of systemic fraud: the manipulation of the indexes that set natural gas prices. As a key form of energy, natural gas is produced, traded, and distributed in the global market. In 2012 Americans consumed between 60 and 90 billion cubic feet of natural gas every day at prices that ranged from $10 to $16 per thousand cubic feet.[1] In a market this large, even small changes in natural gas prices have a significant impact.

The complex market for natural gas essentially involves buyers and sellers linked by traders who negotiate prices and schedules for specific amounts of gas to be delivered on certain dates. Prices can vary significantly across regions and over time, depending on variables like weather conditions. A number of publishing companies collect information on transactions—prices and volume—aggregate the data, and publish the results. These index prices are then used as baseline information in future transactions. In essence, then, the same traders who submit data to the published indexes are also involved in trades that rely on the data. They have every incentive to see those prices move in certain directions given the nature of their transactions. In some transactions they benefit if the price goes up, and in other transactions they benefit if the price goes down.

While there had long been suspicions within the industry about price manipulation, the formal investigation into these concerns began in September 2002 when one of the largest natural gas traders in the United States, Dynegy, announced that some of its employees had routinely provided index publishers with "inaccurate information."[2] Within weeks, most of the other major natural gas trading firms—El Paso, Williams, American Electric Power, CMS—acknowledged that their traders had also submitted fake data to the indexes.[3] In a 2003 report on the manipulation of energy markets, the Federal Energy Regulatory Commission concluded that the reporting of false data to the natural gas price indexes was "epidemic."[4] The institutionalized nature of this practice was revealed by one trader whose boss told him: "this is how the game is played and

---

[1] U.S. Energy Information Agency, "U.S. Natural Gas Consumption," www.eia.gov/forecasts/steo/images/Fig17.png and "U.S. Natural Gas Prices," www.eia.gov/forecasts/steo/images/Fig5.png, October 31, 2013.

[2] Chip Cummins, "Dynegy Disclosure About Data Raises Fresh Questions," *Wall Street Journal*, September 26, 2002.

[3] Chip Cummins, "Misreporting of Energy Prices to Indexes was Commonplace," *Wall Street Journal*. November 19, 2002.

[4] Federal Energy Regulatory Commission, "Final Report on Price Manipulation in Western Markets," Docket No. PA02-2-000, ES6.

you need to play it too."[5] Despite these revelations, only a handful of those individuals directly responsible for the submission of false information were ever prosecuted.

A typical case of fake data submission occurred on July 30, 2002, and involved two employees—Bradley and Martin—of a subsidiary of a large energy company, CMS. According to a complaint filed by the Commodity Futures Transaction Commission (CFTC), on the previous day, Bradley had been contacted by an employee at one of the major indexes, *Gas Daily* (published by Platts, a division of McGraw Hill Financial, which also publishes a widely used index *Inside FERC*) who had asked him for price and volume data on transactions at a natural gas pipeline called Northern TOK. The next day, Bradley telephoned Martin, and in a recorded conversation, they conspired to submit false data.

> BRADLEY: Bob? Hey *Inside FERC* guys are asking me, if I have any indication of Northern TOK prices, to list them. You got an agenda?
>
> MARTIN: I don't know. Should we give them anything?
>
> BRADLEY: It's up to you, if you've already changed your pricing around where you don't have to mess with it, or—
>
> MARTIN: No, we're still TOK-tied on a zillion contracts.
>
> BRADLEY: Well, let's make up some numbers and turn them in.
>
> ....
>
> BRADLEY: You want them low, though.
>
> MARTIN: Oh, yeah.
>
> BRADLEY: How far behind Demarc would you put [the NNTOK price]?
>
> [Demarc is the price point in the published index]
>
> ....
>
> MARTIN: Thirteen cents back of Demarc is what I'd say.[6]

---

[5] *Ibid.*, III-5.

[6] *U.S. Commodities Futures Trading Comm'n v. Jeffrey A. Bradley and Robert L. Martin*, Case No. 05-CV-62-JHP-FHM (NDOK 2005) ("Complaint"), 10.

This was just one of many instances in which Bradley had sent phony data to the index publishers. The CFTC determined that out of 848 transactions for which he submitted information over a four-month period, 261 were fictitious (i.e., involved transactions that never occurred), and 141 represented actual transactions but with altered data.[7]

Natural gas traders at different, and presumably competing, energy companies often conspired to fix natural gas prices. A good example of this type of collusion is seen in a scheme uncovered by the CFTC that involved employees at two energy companies. In July 2000, McDonald worked at the energy firm Mirant in Atlanta and Whalen, who had previously worked with McDonald at Mirant, was employed as a trader at Cinergy Corporation in Houston. The scheme involved an attempt by McDonald to artificially reduce the price on natural gas reported by *Inside FERC* for a particular index (the Permian index). In a phone call with Whalen he attempted to persuade his former colleague to corroborate false transactions he was going to report.

MCDONALD: Yeah, I'm calling about the market. You—I—I'd like a low Permian index. Do you need the same?

WHALEN: Yeah, oh yeah, absolutely.

MCDONALD: I'm going to report a bunch of trades with Cinergy at—I mean I think the Perm index should be down around 370.

WHALEN: Right.

MCDONALD: So I'm going to report a bunch of trades with Cinergy around there.

WHALEN: Ok. Well, I'll do the same.

In a phone conversation the next day the two agreed to compare their submissions to the publishers ahead of time to make their reports more "believable."[8]

---

[7] *Ibid.*, 9.
[8] *U.S. Commodities Futures Trading Comm'n v. Paul Atha, Christopher McDonald and Michael Whalen*, Case No. 1:05-cv-0293-JOF (NDGA 2005) ("Complaint"), 12–13.

One might wonder why the Cinergy trader would have collaborated on a scheme that benefited his firm's competitor, Mirant. The answer is that on other occasions the two colluded on schemes to fabricate data that benefited Cinergy. We will see this same pattern of mutually beneficial collusion among supposed "competitors" in efforts to manipulate Libor interest rates.

The routine submission of false data to the indexes was one of the worst kept secrets in the natural gas trading industry; most insiders were well aware of the fact and took the prices with a grain of salt. One industry insider told the *Houston Chronicle* that the practice "had become not only common but institutionalized." Another commented that the revelations were "no surprise to anyone in the industry; [the practice] was almost kind of a joke."[9] Price manipulation was common knowledge not only among traders but also among the publishers of the indexes themselves. Michelle Markey, who had been in charge of collecting pricing data at two of the major price indexes, told a California legislative panel investigating price manipulation in energy markets: "It was common industry knowledge that exaggeration was part of the process . . . no one acted shocked about the topic."[10]

CALIFORNIA SCHEMING: MANIPULATING MARKETS FOR ELECTRICAL ENERGY

Historically, the production, sale, and distribution of electrical energy was controlled by large public utilities and prices, both retail and wholesale, were set by public regulatory agencies. In the 1990s this model was challenged by a number of critics who claimed that the process was inherently inefficient and led to unnecessarily high consumer prices. One state where this challenge was made successfully was California, where in 1998 the traditional, highly regulated, utility-dominated system was completely replaced by a deregulated system in which electricity was produced, bought, and sold in auctions that were overseen by a state agency,

[9] Michael Davis, "Energy Insiders Say Indictment Reflects Rampant Falsifications," *Houston Chronicle*, December 15, 2002.
[10] Cummins, "Misreporting."

the California Independent System Operator (CAISO), but where the major players were private entities.

The success of this move to deregulate was in no small part the result of the efforts of a new industry, comprised of energy traders, or, as they came to be known, Power Merchants. These were companies that may have begun as producers or distributors of physical commodities like natural gas or electricity but had evolved into purely financial institutions, whose principal activity was speculating in energy markets. The clear industry leader was the Houston-based Enron Corporation, the poster child for the "New Economy." Within months after the new system was established in California, Enron dominated the market, where it was making billions of dollars in profit.

It did not take long for it to become apparent that the new system was not working as intended. The clearest signal that something was wrong came in January 2001 when the state experienced "rolling blackouts" in which electrical power was simply shut off in a number of places in the San Francisco Bay area, leaving people stranded in elevators, and drivers with no traffic lights to guide them. The public outrage that these events provoked became more intense when it was revealed that the blackouts were not caused by actual, physical shortages of electricity but instead had been caused by skyrocketing prices for electrical energy that were the result of strategies by companies like Enron to intentionally game the system. Investigations in the wake of the blackouts revealed that many energy traders—not just Enron's—had engaged in corrupt and sometimes illegal tactics to wring millions of unearned dollars out of a vulnerable system that these companies lobbied to create. These included Enron's infamous "trading strategies" with colorful names like "Get Shorty," "Death Star," and "Fat Boy." Most of these schemes sought to exploit loopholes in the auction process that were put in place to stabilize the market. One of these was a policy that provided "congestion fees" to power companies to not send electricity along lines that were overscheduled at certain times. Traders quickly realized they could reap huge profits from these fees by fabricating load schedules. Later investigations caught traders on tape brazenly discussing these illegal tactics, as in the following conversation between a trader from Public Services Co. of Colorado (PSCo) and a trader from Southern Co. Energy Marketing (SCEM).

SCEM: Hey listen

PSCO: What's up?

SCEM: Here's the deal, er you want um

PSCO: overschedule load at Summit?

SCEM: Yeh . . . I mean like, no no way

PSCO: Smack

SCEM: Hey why not some, we can pick up your 4Cs energy out here and sent it in to NP if you want to trade congestion

PSCO: At Summit through?

SCEM: No, no no no you send in the 4Cs [a quantity of electricity] and we take it up north

PSCO: Yeah dude

SCEM: We collect congestion on about 15 and sell at 26

PSCO: Dude you like rock![11]

Despite sounding like stoned surfers, the two traders were setting up a deal in which they were overscheduling a load of electricity in order to be paid congestion fees.

Conversations like these were part of a mountain of accumulated evidence that revealed that many Power Merchants had systematically employed a wide range of strategies to steal an estimated $8.9 billion from California consumers. Enron's knowledge that it was about to cause a large spike in electrical costs also allowed it to make far larger profits in its trading arms because of insider information about when and how much prices would spike. The reputational damage done to the industry was captured in a 2002 *Fortune* magazine article which asked, "Is Energy Trading a Big Scam?"[12] The industry, which only a few years earlier had been lauded as the cutting edge of the New Economy, was declared by many to be officially dead. But within a few years there were signs of a potential rebirth.

---

[11] Federal Energy Regulatory Commission, "Refiling of Letter and Data from Excel Energy, Inc. in Response to Letter Issued on May 8, 2002 under PA02-2," Docket No. PA-02-2-00, May 23, 2002.

[12] Nelson Schwartz, "Is Energy Trading a Big Scam?" *Fortune*, June 10, 2002.

As the traditional Power Merchants like Enron and Dynegy departed the market, new players were moving in; many of these newcomers were not energy companies but investment banks. In 2002, the Swiss Bank, UBS, purchased Enron's trading unit. By 2004, Wall Street powerhouses like Bear Stearns, Goldman Sachs, Merrill Lynch, and Deutsche Bank had made acquisitions that placed them in the center of energy trading and others soon followed.

One might think that after the scandals surrounding the electrical energy markets in the late 1990s and early 2000s, California authorities would have plugged up all the glaring loopholes in the system. In fact, while some changes were implemented, many openings for fraud remained. These openings were revealed in 2013 when the Federal Energy Regulatory Commission (FERC) took actions against Deutsche Bank Energy LLC, a subsidiary of German financial giant Deutsche Bank, London-based Barclays Bank Plc., and a subsidiary of Wall Street's JP Morgan, all for illegally profiting in California's electrical energy market. Using new powers granted the agency in 2005, FERC imposed some of the largest fines in its history, including $435 million on Barclays and $410 million on JP Morgan. In what follows, we will explore these two cases in detail because they reveal much about the tendency of contemporary financial institutions to pursue profit through the manipulation of rules and the exploitation of inconsistencies in complex markets.

Making Money by Losing Money

Among the many complexities of the California electrical energy market is the fact that it is comprised of not one but several markets, and that market players often participate in all of the markets simultaneously. These facts led many to the simple discovery that one could make money in one market by losing money in another market. This strategy was at the heart of an illegal scheme by Barclays Bank to profit in the energy derivatives market.

In the mid-to-late 2000s, Barclays was a major player in the California electricity market, a significant component of which was the online InterContinental Exchange (ICE), where traders would negotiate contracts to buy and sell electricity in the "day-ahead" market. These transactions involved what were called "physical products" because they require the actual delivery of electricity. Traders who bought and sold in this "next day" market were referred to as "trading dailies." Barclays also bartered in "financial products" in the electricity market, which typically involved what are known as "financial swaps." In essence, these are bets on the direction that electricity prices will take at some point in the future.[13] Both of these markets, for physical products and for financial products, are significantly influenced by prices established by the ICE daily price index. These are baseline prices calculated on the basis of all transactions conducted over specific periods of time.[14]

Exactly how these two markets are related is complicated, but essentially, it is possible that a trader could profit in the market for financial swaps if the index price were artificially depressed or inflated. This could be accomplished if a strategy was employed in the market for "physical products" in which the trader intentionally lost money on a large enough volume of trades. This is exactly what FERC alleged that Barclays did. In a lawsuit the agency alleged that the Barclays traders "engaged in a coordinated scheme during those product months to take the physical positions

---

[13] Federal Energy Regulatory Commission, *Barclays Bank PLC, Daniel Brin, Scott Connelly, Karen Levine, and Ryan Smith*, Docket No. IN08-8-000 ("Enforcement Staff Report and Recommendation"), 2012.

[14] In its complaint against Barclays, FERC described the daily price index in the following way: "One of the most commonly used indices and the relevant one for this case was the Intercontinental Exchange ('ICE') daily index. During the relevant time, much of the electricity trading in the western U.S. occurred on ICE. . . . The ICE daily index was an index published by ICE each trading day based on the VWAP of all day-ahead fixed-price physical electricity transactions at a particular trading location. . . . The ICE daily index was set by a methodology that calculates an index price based on the VWAP of all contributing volumes and prices traded on ICE. The volumes and prices that ICE used to calculate the daily index price were those trades that occurred in the day-ahead fixed-price physical market, a market commonly referred to as the 'cash' or 'dailies' market. In the dailies market, traders bought and sold electricity for physical delivery the following day at fixed prices (e.g., 25 MW/h of peak MIDC electricity for delivery the following day priced at $50 per MW/h)." *U.S. Federal Energy Regulatory Commission v. Barclays Bank; Daniel Brin; Scott Connelly; Karen Levine; and Ryan Smith*, Case 2:13-cv-02093-TLN (EDCA 2013) ("Petition for an Order Affirming the Federal Regulatory Commission's July 16, 2013 Order Assessing Civil Penalties Against Barclays Bank, Daniel Brin, Scott Connelly, Karen Levine, and Ryan Smith"), 6.

they had built and liquidate them in the cash markets—generally at a loss—to impact the ICE daily index settlements to benefit Barclays' related financial positions that settled against those indices."[15] In other words, they were intentionally manipulating one market in order to profit in another market. FERC alleged that over a thirty-five-month period these tactics earned the bank $35 million in unjust profits and cost other market participants $140 million.[16] In July 2013, FERC ordered Barclays to pay a $435 million fine, the largest in FERC's history.

One of the keys to the FERC allegations is the claim that traders knew that they were manipulating the market. In its filings FERC produced numerous email communications as evidence that traders were well aware of the fact that they were engaged in illegal conduct. In one email a trader told another that he was going to "crap on" the day-ahead market in order to lower the daily index which would have the effect of benefiting Barclay's position in financial swaps.[17] In another email a trader used the extreme shorthand of traders to express his intent to manipulate the daily price index in the physical products market to profit in the financial products market: "im [sic]doing phys[ical] so i [sic] am trying to drive price in fin[ancial] direction."[18] In other emails, one trader encouraged another to "prop up" the daily price index and one bragged that he was "going to have fun with the index all month."[19]

In response, Barclays claimed that none of these emails proved intent to manipulate the market but were simply snippets of conversation that FERC had taken out of context and which consisted of "loose, ambiguous and boastful statements" that are common among energy traders. Expressions of "bravado" such as those recorded in the traders' transcripts, Barclays attorneys argued, do not constitute proof of "wrongful conduct."[20] Despite this claim a federal judge in May 2015 allowed the case to proceed.

[15] *FERC v. Barclays Bank*, 8.
[16] *Ibid.*, 8–9.
[17] Erika Kelton, "Barclays' Traders Show How Much Fun Wall Street Has Manipulating Markets," *Forbes*, November 11, 2012.
[18] *FERC v. Barclays Bank*, 15.
[19] *Ibid.*, 18.
[20] *FERC v. Barclays Bank*, ("Answer of Barclays Bank PLC to Order to Show Cause and Notice of Proposed Penalties"), 25.

Money for Nothing

A similar "losing-money-to-make-money" strategy was employed in a scheme by JP Morgan Ventures Energy Corp. to game the electrical energy market. Just two weeks after it assessed penalties on Barclays, in July 2013 FERC ordered the subsidiary of investment bank JP Morgan to pay $410 million in penalties for manipulating electrical energy markets in California and the Midwest.

The complexities of the electrical energy market are mind-boggling, but under the system in place in California the goal is to introduce competition at multiple levels of the market, thereby increasing efficiency and ultimately lowering costs to the consumer. But, at the same time, the system was designed to stabilize the market through a number of mechanisms that decrease volatility and risk to market participants. One of these is what is known as "make-whole payments" which provide additional compensation to generators when their bid price does not cover the costs of generating electricity.

Power generators, the firms that actually produce electrical energy, sell electricity in the "day-ahead market," which, as the name suggests, involves electricity to be delivered the next day, and the "real-time market," which involves the transmission of electricity the same day. Power generators make bids to the CAISO to sell electricity the next day, in specific locations, at specific prices. But, for various reasons, there may be no demand for electricity at that price the next day. For example, if an accepted bid was for $50 a megawatt hour, but the real-time price came in at $30 a megawatt hour, generators would lose money because of the cost of powering up their generators to produce electricity that wasn't actually needed. To compensate them for potential losses, the system's operators (CAISO) would award "make-whole" payments to generators that represented the difference between the "day-ahead" market and the "real-time" market. Significantly, these payments include not only this difference in price but also what is called a "minimum load cost" (the most common form of which is Bid Cost Recovery (BCR)). These "minimum load costs" can be up to twice the actual costs of producing electricity.

FERC alleged that JP Morgan developed a bidding strategy that focused on profiting from these make-whole payments while actually losing money when it produced and sold electricity from two of its power plants.[21] The strategy involved submitting the lowest possible bids in the day-ahead market which would ensure that their bids would be selected. If they actually had to produce electricity at this price they would have lost money. But, under certain conditions, generators are allowed not to actually produce the electricity under the terms of the bid but to buy back the same amount of electricity in the real-time market (i.e., to pay somebody else to generate the electricity). So, for example, if a bid was accepted in the day-ahead market for $30 a megawatt hour (MWh) and the generator was allowed to buy back the electricity at $50 a MWh in the real-time market, they would have technically lost $20 a MWh in the transaction. But, if the generator were awarded minimum-load payments that totaled $70 a MWh, the generator's net gain would be $20 a MWH.[22] Thus, in this greatly simplified example, the power generator would make a substantial profit by not producing any electricity.

FERC and the CAISO claimed that JP Morgan Ventures saw this loophole in the system and devised an entire bidding strategy built around it. In 2008, JP Morgan Chase inherited a number of power plants in California and the Midwest when it purchased the failing investment bank Bear Stearns. Two of those plants were located in Huntington Beach, California, and they utilized outdated technology which made them less efficient, and more expensive to operate . As a result, they frequently lost money. But, under the JPM Ventures bidding scheme they suddenly became profitable. In an eight-month period beginning in August 2010, at the two plants "JPMVEC collected market revenues of $21.9 million for these two plants while spending $29.5 million on gas and operating costs, for a loss at market rates of $7.6 million. But because of $34.6 million in BCR payments, the units generated profits on a marginal cost basis of $27 million over those months. . . ."[23] Based on this pattern of profits FERC

---

[21] Federal Energy Regulatory Commission, 144 FERC ¶ 61,068 ("In Re Make-Whole Payments and Related Bidding Strategies" Docket No. IN11-8-000, 2013.

[22] For a much more detailed description of how this process worked, see California Independent System Operator Corporation, Docket No. ER11-3149-000 ("Tariff Revision and Request for Expedited Treatment. Attachment C—Testimony of Mark Rothleder"), March 25, 2011.

[23] FERC, Docket No. IN11-8-000, 8.

claimed that executives at JP Morgan projected that these previously money-losing plants would generate profits of $1.5 to $2 billion through 2018.[24] In its filings, FERC provided a specific example of how this strategy worked at one plant on a given day.

> On September 22, 2010 for HB4 [one of the Huntington Beach plants], for example, JPMVEC received $143,930 from CAISO in Day Ahead market revenues, and paid $71,968 in the Real Time market. . . . Its market revenues from HB4 were therefore ($143,930 - $71,968 = $71,962). JPMVEC spent $106,567 on gas and operating costs, for a loss of $34,605 at market rates. Because of BCR payments of $159,987, the unit showed a daily profit (on a variable cost basis) of $125,382.[25]

These cases of market misconduct point to a larger trend: increasingly, the financial services industries employ people whose jobs are not to increase their firms' competitiveness or to create better products for their clients but to look for ways to game markets, either legally or illegally. Tyson Slocum of the consumer advocacy group Public Citizen made this point in comments about the JP Morgan case.

> When Wall Street banks engage in electricity trading, they often aren't interested in building value, hiring workers and introducing innovations. Instead, they seek to exploit or create loopholes to bend the market to their advantage. They're not interested in fair competition, but rather twisting the rules to maximize their profits at the expense of honest Americans.[26]

Slocum also pointed out that while the $410 million fine imposed by FERC on JP Morgan may seem like a lot, it represents only 1.2% of the company's 2012 profits.

---

[24] *Ibid.*, 6.
[25] *Ibid.*, 8.
[26] "Get to Know Public Citizen," *Public Citizen News* 33(5) (September/October 2013).

RIGGING LIBOR

The logic of bending rules and manipulating prices and indexes to gain an edge in financial transactions is not limited to the natural gas or electrical energy markets but finds applicability in a wide range of financial markets. It is therefore no coincidence that many of the same investment banks—Barclays, JP Morgan, Deutsche Bank—that were involved in gaming California's energy markets have also been implicated in one of the largest financial scandals in history, the epicenter of which was located over 5,000 miles from California in London, England.

In June 2012 newspapers began to carry articles about an emerging scandal involving something called Libor, the London Interbank Offered Rate. Most people had never heard of Libor, but the media accounts, particularly those in the financial press, seemed to suggest that the Libor scandal was a big deal, a view that was supported when it was reported that Barclays Bank had agreed to pay over $450 million to settle charges by U.K. and U.S. regulators that it had, over a period of at least seven years, manipulated Libor.[27] Despite being little-known to those outside the insular world of investment banks, Libor is an extremely important baseline measure that affects nearly every aspect of the global financial system, from complex financial derivatives to mortgage rates to interest rates on student loans. Approximately *$700 trillion* in derivative contracts around the world are based on Libor.[28] Virtually everyone who has a pension plan was affected. The British Bankers Association, which ran the setting of Libor, called it "The Most Important Number in the World."[29] Banks not only lend money but also borrow money from each other. Libor is a measure of the average amount that banks have to pay each other for loans for set periods of time (e.g., three months) for different currencies. To arrive at the dollar rate, each day at 11 a.m. in London sixteen banks, including Barclays and a number of major U.S. banks, submit estimates

---

[27] Max Colchester and Jeane Eaglesham, "Barclays Settles Rates Probe," *Wall Street Journal*, June 27, 2012.

[28] "Rigged Rates, Rigged Markets," *New York Times*, July 2, 2012.

[29] David Enrich, "British Banks Step Back From Libor Role," *Wall Street Journal*, September 25, 2012.

of their borrowing costs. The higher and lower rates are eliminated and the middle quartiles are then averaged to arrive at that day's Libor rates. Those rates are then used by financial institutions globally to set a baseline for interest rates on all kinds of financial instruments.

In theory, Libor is an objective measure of the real costs of borrowing at major banks. In reality, it turns out, it is just another instrument to be manipulated and gamed as part of schemes to wring unearned profits out of the gigantic global financial system. Barclays employees intentionally manipulated the bank's submissions to Libor for years, in some instances artificially moving the rate in order to affect derivatives transactions and in other instances to give the impression to regulators that the bank's financial health was better than it actually was.

The first type of fraudulent submissions were engineered by derivatives traders whose deals were highly influenced by even small changes in the Libor rate and who would collude with colleagues at their own bank and with their counterparts at other banks to fix the rate in ways that would benefit them. Their collusion was captured in emails obtained by regulators that revealed the casualness with which they would discuss fiddling with the day's rate, as in the following email exchange between a Barclays trader and a Barclays employee responsible for the Libor submission ("Submitter").

> Friday, March 10, 2006:
>
> Trader: "Hi mate[.] We have an unbelievably large set on Monday (the IMM). We need a really low 3m [3-month] fix, it could potentially cost a fortune. Would really appreciate any help, I'm being told by my NYK [boss in New York] that it's extremely important. Thanks."
>
> Monday, March 13, 2006:
>
> Trader: "The big day has[] arrived. . . . My NYK were screaming at me about an unchanged 3m libor. As always, any help wd [would] be greatly appreciated. What do you think you'll go for 3m?" [a three-month Libor rate]

> Submitter: "I am going 90 [4.90%] altho[ugh] 91 is what I
> should be posting."
> Trader: "I agree with you and totally understand. Remember,
> when I retire and write a book about this business your name
> will be in golden letters. . . ."
> Submitter: "I would prefer this not be in any books!"[30]

Barclays's three-month dollar Libor submission on March 13, 2006, was 4.90%, just as the trader had requested. A similar request was made the previous month.

> Trader: "Hi (again) We're getting killed on our 3m resets, we
> need them to be up this week before we roll out of our positions.
> Consensus for 3m today is 4.78 – 4.7825, it would be amazing if
> we could go for 4.79 . . . Really appreciate ur help mate."
> Submitter: "Happy to help."[31]

Barclays's three-month dollar Libor submission on that day was, not surprisingly, 4.79%.

The amount of money riding on these deals and the potential impact of changes in the Libor submission were revealed in the following email exchange.

> Trader 1: "WE WANT TOMORROW'S FIX TO BE 4.07
> MINIMUM," repeating, "4.07. . . . NOTHING LESS. . . . We
> have turn exposure of 837 contracts. [F]or every 0.25 bps
> [basis points] tomorrows [sic] fix is below 4.0525 we lose
> 154,687.50 usd [United States Dollars] . . . if tomorrows [sic]
> fix comes in at 4.0325 we lose 618,750 usd."
> Trader 2: "I'll ask [Submitter-1] to go for 4.07."[32]

---

[30] "Statement of Facts, U.S. Dept. of Justice and Barclays Bank PLC" (June 26, 2012), available at www.justice.gov /iso/opa/resources/9312012710173426365941, 6.

[31] *Ibid.*

[32] *Ibid.*, 9–10.

Translated into plain English, the difference between a submission of 4.07 and a submission of 4.0325 for that day meant a potential loss of over $600,000. Trader 1 got his wish and the submission for that day was 4.07.

In other instances, investigators discovered, Barclays employees colluded with traders at other institutions to manipulate the Libor "fix," as it was known. In the following exchange a former Barclays trader (Trader 1), who was then at another financial institution, requested a rate manipulation from a current Barclays trader (Trader 2).

TRADER 1: "where do u think 3m libor will be today?"

TRADER 2: "[Submitter-1] thinks 38." [5.38%]

TRADER 1: "wow . . . unchanged!!!?!??! Short dates have rallied by 0.75bp . . . So I take it he's going unchanged? If it comes in unchanged I'm a dead man ha ha."

TRADER 2: "i'll [sic] have a chat."

TRADER 1: (later that day): "Dude I owe you big time! Come over one day after work and I'm opening a bottle of Bollinger! Thanks for the libor."

TRADER 2: "know [sic] worries!!!"[33]

While the derivatives traders were often interested in raising the Libor, at other times Barclays management was determined to artificially lower the interest rate. Beginning in late 2008, as the financial crisis began to worsen, regulators were scrutinizing banks like Barclays to determine their health. A relatively high Libor submission would have indicated that the bank had to pay relatively high rates to borrow money, which might have been interpreted as a sign of weak financial health. Senior management wanted very much to avoid that perception because, among other negative consequences, it could have resulted in a declining share price. Investigators uncovered emails from Barclays managers stating that the purpose of the low-ball Libor submissions "was to keep Barclays's 'head below the parapet' so that it did not get 'shot off.'"[34]

---

[33] *Ibid.*, 11.
[34] *Ibid.*, 18.

The participants in the Libor scandal may have included more than just conniving "banksters." There is evidence that regulators on both sides of the Atlantic may have tolerated, and perhaps even encouraged, the manipulation of Libor rates by large banks. In a phone conversation in 2008, a Barclays employee told an analyst at the New York Federal Reserve, the bank's primary regulator in the United States, "We know that we're not posting um, an honest LIBOR . . . and yet we are doing it, because, um, if we didn't do it, it draws, um, unwanted attention on ourselves."[35] Instead of expressing outrage, the Fed analyst expressed sympathy and understanding of the Barclays employee's situation. "You have to accept it . . . I understand. Despite it's against what you would like to do. I understand completely."[36]

The fixing of Libor, like the submission of false data to natural gas price publishers, was an extremely poorly kept secret, if it was a secret at all. Sounding a lot like the chief of police (played by Claude Rains) in the movie *Casablanca* when he tells Humphrey Bogart's character that he was "shocked" to learn of gambling in Bogart's nightclub, Barclays CEO, Robert Diamond, said that he was "angry and disappointed" when he learned of efforts by Barclays employees to manipulate Libor.[37] Yet, if he did not know of the practice, he must have been the only one in the financial industry who did not. In 2007, an article in the *Financial Times* raised questions about the accuracy of the measure, quoting one English banker as saying, the "Libor rates are a bit of a fiction."[38] The next year the *Wall Street Journal* ran a series of articles questioning the validity of Libor, noting that "one of the most important barometers of the world's financial health could be sending false signals."[39] Yet, it took four more years for any official actions to be taken to remedy the situation.

---

[35] Mark Gongloff, "New York Fed's Libor Documents Reveal Cozy Relationship Between Regulators, Banks," *Huffington Post*, July 23, 2012.

[36] *Ibid.*

[37] BBC News, "Libor Scandal: Bob Diamond's Letter to Barclays Staff," July 2, 2012, www .bbc.com/news/business-18678731.

[38] Gillian Tett, "Libor's Value Called into Question," *Financial Times*, September 26, 2007.

[39] Carrick Mollenkamp, "Bankers Cast Doubt on Key Rate Amidst Crisis," *Wall Street Journal*, April 16, 2008.

To many, the Libor scandal may seem like a tempest in a teapot, a situation in which wealthy bankers were stealing from other wealthy bankers. However, it is important to keep in mind the practical consequences of the rate manipulations. Among the many entities that depend on the veracity of Libor are cities, counties, and states that enter into interest rate swap agreements (derivatives) based on Libor as a means of protecting themselves against interest rate increases that would force them to pay higher yields on the bonds they issue. A number of cities discovered that the safety provided by these swaps was false and that fraudulent manipulation of Libor ended up costing them hundreds of millions of dollars. One of those cities was Philadelphia, which in July 2013 filed a lawsuit against a number of large banks claiming that they "artificially and collusively suppressed Libor, which had the effect of secretly tilting the swaps in their favor, causing the banks to be substantially 'in the money' when they did not deserve to be, and effectively raising the losses to The City of Philadelphia."[40] Specifically, the city alleged that these actions forced it to pay $110 million in "termination fees" to unwind the swaps.[41] These losses exacerbated the impact of the financial crisis and led to a severe budget crisis for the city's school district which was forced to lay off teachers and make cuts to music, language, after-school, and gifted programs.[42]

As of this writing, the Philadelphia suit and others like it are winding their way through the courts.[43] Equally significant have been the fines and penalties imposed by regulators and prosecutors both in the United States and abroad, some of which are listed in Table 2.1.

---

[40] *City of Philadelphia v. Bank of Am. Corp., et al.*, Case No. 1:13-cv-06020 (S.D.N.Y. 2013) ("Complaint"), 20.

[41] Reuters, "PhiladelphiaLatestU.S.CitytoSueBigBanksinLiborScandal,"July29,2013,www.reuters.com/article/us-usa-libor-philadelphia-lawsuit-idUSBRE96S0UZ20130729.

[42] Sharon Ward, *Too Big to Trust? Banks, Schools and the Ongoing Problem of Interest Rate Swaps* (Harrisburg, PA: Pennsylvania Budget and Policy Center, 2012), 3.

[43] In March 2013, a federal judge dismissed a class action suit led by the city of Baltimore alleging Libor manipulation. Reuters, "Judge Rejects Much of Libor Lawsuit Against Banks," *New York Times*, March 29, 2013, www.nytimes.com/2013/03/30/business/global/judge-rejects-much-of-libor-lawsuit-against-banks.html.

TABLE 2.1 FINANCIAL INSTITUTIONS SANCTIONED
FOR LIBOR-RIGGING

Institution	Year of Action	Penalty/Fine	Headquarters
Barclays Bank	2012	450,000,000	U.K.
UBS	2012	1,500,000,000	Switzerland
Royal Bank of Scotland	2013	612,000,000	U.K.
ICAP	2013	87,000,000	U.K.
Rabobank	2013	1,000,000,000	Netherlands
UBS AG	2013	800,000,000	Switzerland
J.P. Morgan	2013	108,000,000	U.S.
Citigroup	2013	96,000,000	U.S.
Deutsche Bank	2013	980,000,000	Germany
Royal Bank of Scotland	2013	530,000,000	U.K.
Societe Generale	2013	604,417,450	France
RP Martin	2013	2,200,000	U.K.
Lloyds Bank	2014	380,000,000	U.K.
J.P. Morgan	2014	82,230,000	
Royal Bank of Scotland	2014	0	U.K.
Deutsche Bank	2015	2,500,000,000	Germany

Source: "Tracking the Libor Scandal," *New York Times.* April 23, 2015.

FOREX SCANDAL

In May 2015 four of the world's largest banks—Citigroup, JP Morgan Chase, Barclays, and Royal Bank of Scotland—agreed to plead guilty to

U.S. felony charges for their efforts to manipulate foreign exchange rates over a period of years.[44] It was a rare occasion in which large banks were not simply let off the hook with fines and deferred prosecution agreements but were hit with criminal sanctions for their financial crimes. The banks, however, were exempted from what would normally have been the serious consequences of guilty pleas—the loss of their licenses to do business in the United States. In addition to their convictions, the banks agreed to pay fines totaling $2.5 billion.

Most of us are aware of currency exchange rates only when we travel abroad and see the rates offered at the money-changing outlets in airports and elsewhere. However, foreign exchange or Forex markets are huge, with $5.3 trillion changing hands every day. Currencies are traded round-the-clock and the rates vary throughout the day. But in order to create a benchmark rate for all trades, at 4:00 London time every weekday, the transactions for the most frequently traded currencies, including the U.S. dollar and the Euro, are monitored for sixty seconds and a median exchange rate is calculated or "fixed," at that becomes known as the "fix rate" or the "WM/R fix rate." Another bench rate, known as the "ECB fix," is calculated at 1:15 London time every weekday. Investors, who include banks, investment firms, hedge funds, will often place orders to buy or sell certain currencies at the "fix rate" for a given day. The orders are placed with banks which agree to buy or sell to clients at the specified fix rate. At the same time, the bank's traders are also buying selling currencies at rates that float up and down throughout the day. The banks make money if their traders are able to buy currencies at rates that, on average, are lower than the fix rates for their sell orders, or if they are able to sell currencies at rates that are lower than fix

---

[44] A fifth bank, UBS, was also accused of Forex manipulation but was not charged with criminal violations but did agree to plead guilty to charges involving Libor manipulation. In her press conference announcing the charges Assistant Attorney General Janet Caldwell specifically cited the bank's violation of its Libor-related deferred prosecution agreement, stating: "UBS has a 'rap sheet' that cannot be ignored. Within the past six years, the department has resolved criminal investigations of UBS three times, resulting in non-prosecution or deferred prosecution agreements. . . . Enough is enough." U.S. Department of Justice. "Assistant Attorney General Leslie R. Caldwell Delivers Remarks at a Press Conference on Foreign Exchange Spot Market Manipulation," news release, May 20, 2015, www.justice.gov/opa/speech/assistant-attorney-general-leslie-r-caldwell-delivers-remarks-press-conference-foreign.

rates for buy orders. This gives the traders significant incentives to attempt to manipulate the daily fix rates. But this can only happen if they are able to coordinate with traders from other banks so that their trades don't counteract each other. The FX market is dominated by traders at a small number of large international banks, so that if they were to collude with each other they could drive the fix rate in one direction or the other. This is exactly what they did. By buying or selling large amounts of currencies just before or during the fix period, traders were able to manipulate the fix rate up or down, while the other traders would stay out of their way.

The traders at different banks communicated with one another in electronic chat rooms that had colorful names like "the Cartel" and "Bandits' Club." Using coded shorthand, the traders would discuss their trades and strategies for rigging the fix rate. In the exchange that follows, a trader from JP Morgan Chase (JPMC) is discussing with a trader at an undisclosed bank (Bank X) a plan to manipulate the 4 p.m. "fix rate" just before the fix period.

JPMC Trader:	3:52:39	tell u what
	3:52:42	let's double team it
	3:52:45	how much I got
Bank X Trader:	3:52:46	ok
	3:52:47	300
	3:52:45	u?
JPMC Trader:	3:53:01	ok i'll give you 500 more
Bank X Trader:	3:53:05	wow
	3:53:06	ok
	3:53:08	ha
	3:53:09	cool...
JPMC Trader:	3:53:20	so we have 800 each
	3:53:21	ok
	3:53:31	but we gotta both do some at fix
	3:53:36	don't sell them all and take foot off haha
Bank X Trader:	3:53:40	i promise i will
JPMC Trader:	3:53:47	me too[45]

---

[45] *In re J.P. Morgan Chase*, USA Before the Commodities Futures Trading Commission, Docket No. 15-04, 2014 ("Order Instituting Proceedings"), 7–8.

Leaving aside the jargon, the traders are clearly colluding to rig the fix rate. Here they are agreeing to buy and sell each other euros in order to alter that day's rate. The traders are ostensibly competitors and the market is supposed to prosper from their competition, providing investors with the best prices. Their collaboration undermines this premise and investors are the ultimate losers.

The currency traders were clearly aware of the illicit nature of their schemes and took precautions to hide their collusion. In one chat room exchange a JP Morgan trader warned others about the need to maintain secrecy in a discussion about whether to admit another trader to their circle:

JPMC Trader:	7:51:16	You know him
	7:51:21	Will he tell rest of desk stuff
	7:51:26	Or God forbid his NYK [boss in New York]?
Bank X Trader:	7:51:46	yes
	7:51:51	that's really imp[ortant] q[uestion]
	7:52:01	don't want other numpty's in market to know
	7:52:17	but not only that
	7:52:21	is he gonna protect us
	7:52:33	like we protect each other . . .[46]

The trader was ultimately admitted to the group for a one-month "trial." But the Bank X trader warned him: "mess this up and sleep with one eye open at night."[47]

These individual transactions did not result in huge profits. A suit filed by the New York State regulators against Barclays describes a series of transactions by a trader in a single day in which the fix rate was rigged that produced profits of $16,000, another trade that netted the bank $14,200, another in which the bank earned $59,000.[48] But these profits added up, as

---

[46] Ibid., 5–6.
[47] Ibid., 6.
[48] New York State Department of Financial Services, In re Barclays Bank, PLC ("Consent Order"), May 20, 2015, 9–10.

the traders were doing these deals daily over a period of years and earning millions of dollars for their employers and themselves.

As in the Libor-rigging cases, these were not rogue traders acting on their own, while keeping their superiors in the dark about their collusive and illegal behavior. Rather, as the regulators and prosecutors point out in their formal accusations, the roots of these financial crimes were "systemic." In its settlement with Barclays Bank, The New York State Department of Financial Services' asserted that: "the misconduct at the Bank was systemic and involved various levels of employees. . . . The culture within the Bank valued increased profits with little regard to the integrity of the market."[49] As an example, the document cites a 2012 statement by a senior FX trader that "Large fixes are the key to making money as we have more chances of moving the market our way." The trader then announced a new "added incentive" program in which traders would earn 50% of the profits for "increasing trading volume at certain fix orders."[50] Moreover, despite the negative publicity surrounding its traders' involvement in the Libor-rigging scandal, in May 2012, the bank did not begin an investigation into the Forex traders' misconduct until June 2013, after *Bloomberg News* published an article exposing their practices.[51]

DISCUSSION

At the heart of our contemporary financial markets lies the economic assumption that these systems function efficiently because participants respond rationally to "signals" being emitted by the system. According to economic theory, these signals include things like interest rates, foreign exchange rates, and natural gas and electrical energy prices. These signals are assumed to have an objective quality, which, like measures of rainfall or the movement of glaciers, are unaffected by human behavior. What we have stressed repeatedly in this chapter is that these "signals" are in fact social constructs, the practical accomplishments of individuals in

---

[49] New York State Department of Financial Services, *In re Barclays . . .*, 16.
[50] *Ibid.*
[51] *Ibid.*, 17–18.

specific social settings that are governed by their own norms of behavior.[52] Just like in the *Wizard of Oz* when Dorothy pulls back the curtain in the Emerald City and discovers not the "Great and Powerful Oz" but an old man pushing buttons and pulling levers, once you pull back the curtains of the financial system you find real, live human beings making phone calls, sending emails, texting one another in more or less overt attempts to manipulate the marketplace. The conflict between economic theory and reality comes down to the fact that the people who actually operate in these environments are not motivated by a desire to create more efficient and rational markets but by a desire to make money, for themselves and for their employers, and will quickly figure out ways to succeed by colluding to bend rules and manipulate data.

[52] This view of financial markets is consistent with the growing literature in the sociology of financial markets. See Karin Knorr-Cetina and Alex Preda, eds., *The Oxford Handbook of the Sociology of Finance* (New York: Oxford University Press, 2012).

[3]

FAKING IT WITH ACCOUNTING TRICKS

In a speech given in 1998, Arthur Levitt, then chairman of the Securities and Exchange Commission (SEC), warned that a "numbers game" was being played in the business world.

> Too many corporate managers, auditors, and analysts are participants in a game of nods and winks. In the zeal to satisfy consensus earnings estimates and project a smooth earnings path, wishful thinking may be winning the day over faithful representation. . . . Managing may be giving way to manipulation; Integrity may be losing out to illusion.[1]

Levitt's warning came amidst accounting scandals at several large corporations, including Cendant, where disclosures about financial misreporting caused the firm's stock to lose half of its value in a single day and caused holders of its shares to lose $14 billion.[2] But the worst was yet to come. Beginning in the fall of 2001 with Enron's collapse and continuing through the following year, Americans were exposed to a stream of revelations about financial frauds at some of the country's largest and seemingly most successful companies. High-flying New Economy firms like Enron, WorldCom, and Global Crossing became engulfed in scandal.

---

[1] Arthur Levitt, "The 'Numbers Game'" (speech given to the NYU Center for Law and Business, New York City, September 28, 1998), www.sec.gov/news/speech/speecharchive/1998/spch220.txt.

[2] Gretchen Morgenson, "Before Enron, there was Cendant," *New York Times* May 9, 2004.

The scope of the phenomenon was reflected in two statistical indicators: financial restatements and class action securities fraud suits, both of which rose significantly in the latter part of the 1990s. Between 1997 and 2002, nearly 10% of the firms listed on the three major stock exchanges announced plans to file restatements.[3] Over the next three years, the rate of restatement announcements increased so that in the period 2002–2005 nearly 16% of all companies listed on the three exchanges announced restatements.[4] In roughly the same time period (1997–2005), over 2,200 class action law suits alleging securities fraud were filed in federal courts.[5] The publicity surrounding corporate scandals also had the effect of significantly reducing investor confidence. Polls found that by July 2002, 40% of those individuals interviewed said they were less likely to invest in stocks because of accounting frauds.[6]

Several studies provide a basis for determining the broader impact of corporate corruption on the economy and on ordinary individuals. For example, researchers at the Brookings Institution calculated that the corporate scandals that began with Enron's bankruptcy in December 2001 and ended with WorldCom's bankruptcy announcement in July 2002 resulted in a loss of $35 billion in the gross domestic product (GDP).[7] Using a similar methodology, the New York State Office of the Comptroller estimated that the scandals cost the retirement fund for state and municipal employees $9 billion. The impacts this had on pension participants were sudden and dramatic. The average plan participant in his or her sixties lost an estimated $10,450 from his or her account in just a four-month period as a result of the decline in the value of stock from corrupt corporations.[8]

[3] General Accounting Office, *Financial Statement Restatements: Trends, Market Impacts, Regulatory Responses, and Remaining Challenges* (GAO-03-138) (Washington, DC: U.S. Government Printing Office, 2002).

[4] Government Accountability Office, *Financial Restatements: Update of Public Company Trends, Market Impacts, and Regulatory Enforcement Activities* (GAO-06-678) (Washington, DC: U.S. Government Printing Office, 2006).

[5] Securities Class Action Clearing House, "Indices of Securities Class Action Filings" (Palo Alto, CA: Stanford University, 2007), http://securities.stanford.edu/litigation_activity.html.

[6] General Accounting Office, *Financial Statement Restatements*, 34.

[7] Carol Graham, Robert Litan and Sandip Sukhtankar, "Cooking the Books: The Cost to the Economy," Brookings Institute, 2002, www.brookings.edu/research/papers/2002/08/business-graham.

[8] New York State Office of the Comptroller, *Impact of the Corporate Scandals on New York State* (Albany, NY: Office of the State Comptroller, 2003).

In a 2007 study, Tillman and Indergaard took a closer look at the firms in the Government Accounting Office (GAO) sample that had been specifically accused of fraud, either by the SEC or in class action lawsuits by shareholders. They found that nearly half (45%) had been accused of fraud and that losses to investors (as measured by change in market capitalization immediately following the restatement announcement) totaled $84 billion. In the great majority of these accusations, the people at the top of the companies—chief executive officers (CEOs) and chief financial officers (CFOs)—were specifically named as being responsible for fraudulent activities. But they were not alone. In the majority of lawsuits and SEC actions individuals from outside the company—board members, auditors, and bankers—were also named as defendants. This is significant because these are *the very people who the public had been assured could be relied upon to serve as corporate watchdogs, to monitor and prevent fraud*, but who were now colluding with their corporate clients to defraud investors. All five of the top accounting firms in the United States were named as defendants multiple times, and one, Price Waterhouse, was named in eighteen different legal actions. Yet, only one of those five accounting firms, Enron's outside auditor Arthur Andersen, was ever charged with a crime for its involvement in that firm's massive corporate accounting fraud.[9]

These findings on the extent of involvement by outsiders in corporate accounting fraud challenged the traditional "free market" view, favored by many economists, which held that these outsiders—accountants, lawyers, bankers—are deterred from colluding with corporate insiders in fraudulent schemes by fear of the "reputational penalty" they will suffer if their collusion is discovered. If that were to happen their reputations would be tainted, potential clients would avoid them, and their material interests would be severely damaged.[10] An early proponent of this view was Alan Greenspan, a powerful chairman of the Federal Reserve, who was forced to rethink his views after the scandals at Enron and many other

---

[9] Robert Tillman and Michael Indergaard, *Control Overrides in Financial Statement Fraud: A Report to the Institute for Fraud Prevention* (2007), www.theifp.org/research-grants/control%20overrides_final.pdf.

[10] Robert Tillman, "Reputations and Corporate Malfeasance," *Crime, Law and Social Change* 51 (2009).

major corporations in the early 2000s. As he told a congressional panel in 2002:

> [M]y view was always that accountants basically knew or had to know that the market value of their companies rested on the integrity of their operations . . . and that, therefore, their self-interest is so strongly directed at making certain that their reputation was unimpeachable, that regulation by Government was utterly unnecessary, and indeed, most inappropriate. *I was wrong*[11] (emphasis added).

In contrast to this view, a number of criminologists and legal scholars have argued that collusive accounting fraud strategies have become more and more common because of larger changes in the corporate environment. As accountants, lawyers, and bankers came to see themselves as "consultants and partners" of their corporate clients rather than outside auditor/monitors,[12] as changes in securities law made it more difficult for shareholders to sue the companies whose shares they held,[13] and as accounting and law firms began to reduce their legal exposure by organizing as limited liability partnerships,[14] collaborating with executives in fraudulent accounting schemes superseded concerns about "reputational costs" and made more financial sense. William Black has argued that accounting fraud is an "optimal strategy" for many white-collar crimes because:

> it simultaneously produces record (albeit fictional) profits and prevents the recognition of real losses. This combination reduces the risk of detection and successful prosecution

---

[11] "Federal Reserve's Second Monetary Policy Report for 2002," Senate Comm. on Banking, Housing and Urban Affairs, 107th Cong. (2002), 32.

[12] John Coffee, "What Caused Enron? A Capsule Social and Economic History of the 1990s," *Cornell Law Review* 89 (2004).

[13] Robert H. Tillman and Michael L. Indergaard, *Pump and Dump* (New Brunswick, NJ: Rutgers University Press, 2005), 174–175.

[14] Jonathan Glater, "Fearing Liability, Law Firms Change Partnership Status" *New York Times*, January 10, 2003; Jonathan Macy and Hillary Sale, "Observations on the Role of Commodification, Independence, and Governance in the Accounting Industry," *Villanova Law Review* 48 (2003).

> because the CEO can use normal corporate mechanisms (e.g., raises, bonuses, stock options, dividends and appreciation in the value of the firm's stock) to convert the creditor's funds to his personal use. The blessing by the top tier audit firm of the fictional profits provides "cover" to the CEO against fraud prosecutions that would never exist were he simply to embezzle funds.[15]

Corporate players are organized to present a collective charade in which auditors, boards of directors, law firms, and regulators are often allies of corporate executives who utilize them to "'mimic' a robustly healthy, legitimate firm."[16]

In this chapter we take a closer look at several instances of corporate accounting fraud. We will start with the well-known case of Enron, where the abuses and corruption were particularly egregious. We then turn our attention to more recent and lesser known cases of financial statement fraud involving foreign companies operating in "hot" markets and whose stocks were traded on American exchanges.

ENRON

At the heart of many New Economy schemes to defraud investors were accounting tricks that caused corporate debt to either disappear or be magically transformed into assets and created fictional income. The magicians who performed these illusions worked for the Big Four accounting firms which had shed their roles as independent auditors and taken on the role of consultants to their clients. In many cases, accountants devised ways for firms to be in technical compliance with accounting rules with financial arrangements that made a mockery of the substance of the rules. For example, WorldCom's accounting of its huge merger deals made it appear as if its revenues were continually rising while its costs were dropping—a

---

[15] William Black, "'Control Frauds' as Financial Super-Predators," *The Journal of Socio-Economics* 34(6) (2005): 734–755.
[16] *Ibid.*, 737.

ruse which set an unobtainable standard for other telecoms, many of which, in turn, engaged in fraud to keep up with the leader. Enron was arguably the most aggressive player when it came to gaming the rules; many of the deceptive accounting practices came to light after the fall of Enron when investigators began looking at how accounting firms had colluded with company insiders to, in essence, "cook the books."

Investigators learned that the energy company had for years grossly inflated its revenues by utilizing an accounting method known as "mark-to-market" under which a firm can record all future revenues and profit from an energy contract in the quarter in which the contract was signed. Rather than recording revenues and profits (as well as any losses on the deal) as they came in, mark-to-market rules were abused to allow energy companies to record as revenue on their annual financial statements the entire amount of an energy contract. An example of such an accounting abuse occurred when Enron signed a contract to sell $1 million worth of natural gas, but even though Enron also had to buy the same amount of gas for $900,000 in order to resell it, the company recorded the entire $1 million as revenue. Abusing mark-to-market accounting allowed Enron to pump up its revenues–and stock price—dramatically. Had appropriate accounting standards been applied, the $101 billion in revenues that Enron reported in 2001 would have turned into $6.3 billion and the company that claimed to be the seventh largest corporation in America would have dropped to 287th in the rankings.[17]

The primary means by which Enron created fictional profits and hid real debt was by making phony "sales" of assets (and transferring debt) to "special purpose entities," which removed the debt from Enron's balance sheet. In 2000, the year that saw Enron's stock price peak, the energy company used these tactics to erase $10 billion of debt from its balance sheet. In these financial shell games, Enron executives would create a partnership as part of a "special purpose entity" and then transfer a poorly performing debt-ridden asset to the partnership, which removed the debt from the balance sheets.

At least 3% of the entity had to be owned by independent outsiders, otherwise the partnership's finances had to be included on Enron's statements.

That would mean (1) that it could not book the (fictional) profit on the (fictional) "sale" of its (fictional) "assets" and (2) could not take the (very real) debts off Enron's balance sheet. That would mean that Enron would have to report the truth–it was deeply insolvent and unprofitable. That would mean it would be bankrupt and its officers would lose the massive bonuses that they got for creating the fictional income through scam "sales." But these supposedly "independent" outsiders were part of the scam and did not provide even the trivial 3% of the (fictional) capital.

Because no truly independent party would put up even 3% of the special purpose entities' (fictional) capital, Enron's CFO arranged a scam with Wall Street commercial and investment banks that desperately wanted Enron's business.[18] Enron, secretly, agreed with the banks that although their "capital" contribution was not real–Enron would bear any losses. With these financial sleights of hand Enron executives were able get very wealthy by creating the illusion of a successful company.

Perhaps a not-so-obvious question concerns the Enron executives' motives. Why would they risk their careers to build a company that was essentially a house of cards and destined to collapse? The answer is simple: they made a lot of money in the process. Enron was well-known for paying its top executives lavishly and a significant part of their compensation came in the form of stock options which gave them the ability to purchase the company's stock at a future date at the current date's price. Thus, if the stock price increased, their options increased in value. Between 1998 and 2000, the top 200 employees received over $1.3 billion in compensation from stock options.[19] This gave them every incentive to artificially "pump up" the value of Enron's stock, and then sell, or "dump," the stock before the true value of the company was realized and the stock price plummeted. In a three-year period from October 19, 1998, to November 27, 2001, twenty-nine Enron insiders sold a total of $1.1 billion of their company's stock. Among those was CEO Kenneth Lay, who sold $101 million in Enron shares; Jeffrey Skilling, the company's chief operating officer (COO), who cashed out $66 million in stock; and CFO Andrew Fastow,

[18] *Ibid.*, 87.
[19] *Ibid.*, 93.

who sold "a mere" $30 million of his Enron stock. The truly big money, though, went to Lou Pai, CEO of a subsidiary, Enron Accelerator, who sold off $353 million worth of Enron stock during the period.[20]

By contrast, those Enron shareholders who were outside Enron's inner circles, and who were kept in the dark about the company's true condition, watched the value of their investments decline to virtually nothing. In 2000, Enron's market capitalization (the value of all outstanding shares) peaked at $70 billion. By late November 2001, after revelations about Enron's numerous scams had begun to emerge, that number had plummeted to less than $1 billion. In other words, it took just over a year for $69 billion in investors' wealth to evaporate into thin air.[21] These shareholders included not just individual investors but also Enron employees who bought stock as part of the company's 401k plan and a stock ownership plan, and individuals who owned Enron stock indirectly through mutual funds and pension plans. Included in this latter group were New York City employees who lost an estimated $109 million from their pensions when Enron collapsed.[22] Florida state employees (whose fund manager bought 2.7 million shares of Enron stock just weeks before the company declared bankruptcy) watched as $300 million vanished from their pension fund. State employees in Alabama saw the value of their pension fund decline by $65 million when Enron declared bankruptcy.[23]

One of the striking features of the Enron saga was the speed with which the fortunes of the company and its executives were completely reversed. In April 2000, the author of a *Fortune* magazine article gushed over the company, comparing its impact on the energy industry to the influence that Elvis Presley had on popular music. In that same year a book entitled *Leading the Revolution* described Enron's executives as "gray-haired revolutionaries" and praised the company for 'institutionaliz[ing] a capacity for perpetual innovation."[24] By the end of the following year,

---

[20] *Ibid.*
[21] *Ibid.*, 85.
[22] *Ibid.*, 94.
[23] *Ibid.*
[24] Gary Hamel, *Leading the Revolution* (Boston: Harvard Business School Press, 2000), 216–217.

2001, everything had changed; the doors of the company's Houston headquarters were locked and thousands of its former employees were out of work. The speed of these changes reflects the mercurial nature of boom-and-bust economies in which today's business visionaries are tomorrow's villains, appearing on the covers of business magazines one day and then in handcuffs doing perp-walks on the front page of national newspapers the next. In these rapidly changing environments companies that appear to be on the cutting edge of the economy may simply be cutting and pasting together a series of lies in order to deceive investors.

INDIA'S ENRON

On January 7, 2009, Ramalinga Raju, chairman of the giant Indian outsourcing firm Satyam Computer Services, wrote a letter to the company's directors in which he admitted that he had systematically inflated revenues at the company for years so that 94% of the company's cash on the books, $1 billion, was fictitious. At the same time he and others had systematically understated the company's liabilities, thereby showing very strong profits. The methods for creating the fake revenues were fairly simple. Raju and others had created thousands of phony invoices over the years for services they never provided and for customers that did not exist. The purpose of the inflated revenues was to make the company's growth appear spectacular, which in turn helped to attract clients and, more important, investments and loans to the company. In Raju's letter of confession he claimed that initially the creation of a false performance picture was intended to stave off a takeover of the company by outsiders, but as time went on the gap between the actual numbers and the fake numbers grew larger and impossible to reconcile. As he put it: "It was like riding a tiger, not knowing how to get off without being eaten."[25] In his letter he emphasized that "neither me, nor the Managing Director took even one rupee/dollar from the company and have not benefitted in financial terms on account of the inflated results."[26]

[25] "Satyam fraud: Full text of Raju's letter to board," *Financial Express,* January 7, 2009, http://archive.financialexpress.com/news/satyam-fraud-full-text-of-rajus-letter-to-board/407799.
[26] *Ibid.*

An investigation by India's Central Bureau of Investigation (CBI) came to a different conclusion about the motives behind the scheme. Taking a page out of the Enron playbook, the top officers at Satyam took advantage of the company's rising stock price to "make hay while the sun was shining, offloading the shares, while the other investors might have been holding on to the shares with a false hope of an increase in their values."[27] In another component of the illicit scheme, company insiders and their relatives created 327 investment companies, transferred shares of Satyam into those companies, and then used those shares to collateralize loans which in turn were used to invest in real estate and agricultural ventures.[28] Prosecutors estimated that, in total, Raju and his confederates caused shareholders to lose $2.25 billion when the value of their stock plummeted.[29] In November2009, Indian prosecutors filed a criminal complaint against Raju and 212 business associates and relatives charging them with money laundering.

Almost immediately after Raju's confession became public, the media began referring to Satyam as "India's Enron." The parallels between the two scandal-ridden companies are indeed striking and the similarities suggest something about the underlying conditions that are conducive to financial statement fraud.

Both companies, Satyam and Enron, grew rapidly by utilizing new technologies to gain advantages in swiftly changing environments. Enron began in the 1980s as the owner and operator of natural gas pipelines and rode a wave of deregulation in the natural gas and electrical energy markets in the 1990s to become a paragon of the New Economy, a self-proclaimed "knowledge based company" whose primary business was trading rather than creating or moving physical products. It was also part of the larger trend toward financialization. Just before its collapse, Paul Krugman, *New*

---

[27] CBI, Chargesheet against Satyam, Paragraph 63, April 7, 2009, Provided as an attachment to: Heather Timmons, "Report Details Broad Scope of Fraud at Satyam," *New York Times*, April 21, 2009, www.nytimes.com/2009/04/22/business/22satyam.html.

[28] *Ibid.*, para. 67.

[29] AFP, "Ex-Satyam chief gets seven years for 'India's Enron,'" *Daily Mail*, April 9, 2015, www.dailymail.co.uk/wires/afp/article-3031570/India-court-convicts-ex-Satyam-chief-2-25-bln-fraud-case.html.

York Times columnist and Nobel Prize-winning Distinguished Professor, described the company as in the "vanguard of a powerful movement that hopes to 'financialize' (Enron's term) just about everything—that is, trade almost everything as if it were stock options."[30] Enron's reported assets grew from just under $12 billion in 1994 to over $65 billion in 2000, a year in which it had over 20,000 employees.[31] In India, Satyam followed a similar trajectory. Begun in Hyderabad, India with twenty employees in 1987 by two brothers, the company became an early leader in the out-sourcing industry which saw explosive growth in the 1990s as American firms perceived the value in contracting out their software problems and back-office functions to companies with low labor costs in countries like India. By 2008, the firm was reporting revenues in excess of $2 billion and had 53,000 employees with operations in sixty-six countries. Its clients included many large American corporations including General Electric, General Motors, and Nestle.[32] Rapid growth often masks corporate fraud by reducing investors' and regulators' incentives to investigate suspicious transactions and anomalies in apparently robust financial statements. Warren Buffet, the American investment guru, has often been quoted as saying: "When the tide goes out you see who's been swimming naked."

Before their falls, both companies were the darlings of the business media; the firms and their officers were recipients of numerous awards and special recognitions. In 2007, Ernst & Young awarded Ramalinga Raju its "Entrepreneur of the Year Award." In 2008, just four months before Raju's confession, the World Council on Corporate Governance gave Satyam its "Golden Peacock Award" for excellence in corporate governance. Satyam gained more positive publicity when it announced that it had become an official sponsor for the World Cup Soccer matches in 2010 and 2014.[33] Here too, the Indian firm was following in the path of Enron. In the 1990s, Enron was named *Fortune* magazine's "Most Innovative Company" six years in a row and in 1999, two years before the firm imploded, CFO Andy

---

[30] Paul Krugman, "Enron Goes Overboard," *New York Times*, August 18, 2001.

[31] Mergent Online, database.

[32] Heather Timmons and Bettina Wasser, "Satyam Chief Admits Huge Fraud," *New York Times*, January 7, 2009.

[33] Floyd Norris, "A Corporate Hero Admits Fraud," *New York Times*, January 7, 2009.

Fastow was given a "CFO Excellence Award" by *CFO* magazine.[34] Two years before its collapse, the firm also sought to enhance its public image by aligning its name with sports when it bought the naming rights for $100 million and the Houston Astros began playing baseball in Enron Field.[35] The CEOs of both firms had built solid reputations for their involvement in charitable activities. For Enron's Kenneth Lay it was primarily the Ken Lay Family Foundation which gave generously to local causes.[36] For Raju it was his Byrraju Foundation which provided assistance to schools and health care systems in poor, rural areas in India.[37] Ironically, these types of awards, publicity campaigns, and good deeds may actually further corporate fraud by allowing companies to burnish their public image, providing them with a cloak of respectability that shields them from scrutiny and allows them to prolong their fraudulent schemes. Indeed, as we have seen, some of the most costly control frauds effectively suborn internal and external controls in order to continue to profit illegally over a long period of time. Obtaining accolades from outside the firm effectively prevents impugning both the reputation and seeming legitimacy that such awards inevitably produce, and are an important element in all major control frauds.

Finally, in both cases a lot of people went to jail. Over thirty former Enron employees were eventually charged with crimes, including former top executive Jeff Skilling who was initially sentenced to twenty-four years in prison and former CFO Andy Fastow who received a ten-year sentence. CEO Ken Lay was convicted but suffered a fatal heart attack before being sentenced. In India, nineteen Satyam employees, including Raju's wife and sons, were convicted of crimes associated with the scandal and received prison sentences of a year and a half. Ironically, Raju and his brother were eventually sentenced to seven years in prison for their roles in the scandal, but their sentences were suspended.[38]

[34] Bethany McLean and Peter Elkind, *The Smartest Guys in the Room* (New York: Penguin, 2004), 155, 239.

[35] Tillman and Indergaard, *Pump and Dump*, 274.

[36] McLean and Elkins, *Smartest Guys*, 86.

[37] Elizabeth Corcoran, "The Seeds of the Satyam Scandal," *Forbes*, January 8, 2009.

[38] Press Trust of India, "Satyam Scam: Ramalinga Raju, 9 Others Get Bail, Sentence Suspended," *The Indian Express*, May 11, 2015, http://indianexpress.com/article/india/india-others/satyam-fraud-case-ramalinga-raju-9-other-get-bail-sentence-suspended/.

Even in his letter of confession Raju apparently lied when he wrote that he had not "benefitted in financial terms on account of the inflated results." But regulators and prosecutors later claimed that Raju and his cronies made illegal profits of over $300 million by selling their company stock at prices inflated by their accounting manipulations.[39] This was perhaps the ultimate irony for a firm whose name, in Sanskrit, means "truth."

OLYMPUS AND THE ART OF *ZAITECH* ‑Japan

In June 2011, the Olympus Corporation was one of Japan's premier companies. With a solid international reputation as a maker of consumer cameras it was also the dominant manufacturer of endoscopes, the optical device used in medical procedures around the world. Its stock was selling on the Tokyo Stock Exchange for ¥2,500 a share. Four months later the company's reputation was in tatters, its stock price had declined to ¥500 per share, and its executive suites were in turmoil. The sudden shift in the company's fortunes began in August 2011 when a small Japanese business magazine published a series of articles alleging, among other things, that Olympus had made excessive payments to a firm involved in Olympus's acquisition of a much smaller company. After first denying the accusations, in early November the company released a statement acknowledging that the company had for many years been hiding corporate losses from investors.[40] Shortly thereafter investigations were begun by authorities in Japan and the United States and in 2012 the former chairman of the board, a former vice president, and the former chief auditor for the firm pled guilty in a Japanese court to charges of securities fraud.

At its core the Olympus scandal is a story about the consequences of financialization in a Japanese context, but with Western influences. It is a story about a company that took a gamble by shifting its focus from

---

[39] "Raju, "Kin Made Rs 2,000 Crore in Satyam Scam," *The Times of India*, August 22, 2014, http://timesofindia.indiatimes.com/city/hyderabad/Raju-kin-made-Rs-2000-crore-in-Satyam-scam-Sebi/articleshow/40628978.cms.

[40] Hiroko Tabuchi, "Olympus Hid Investing Losses in Big Merger Payouts," *New York Times*, November 7, 2011.

manufacturing to "financial engineering," lost a lot of money, and then engaged in a decades-long accounting fraud to cover up those losses. At the center of the scandal was a small group of executives who had extensive ties to securities firms, politicians, and even organized crime groups. The close ties among these executives and the traditional secrecy in which Japanese corporations operate made it possible to perpetrate this fraud for many years before it was revealed.

Throughout the 1980s the Japanese economy expanded rapidly as Japanese consumer goods like automobiles and electronics were hugely successful exports to countries like the United States. But the beginning of the end of this boom came in 1985 when the United States and Japan signed the Plaza Accord (so-called because it was signed in the Plaza Hotel in New York), which brought down the value of the dollar, thereby dramatically reducing the profits of Japanese exporters.[41] To make up for this decline in profits, Olympus began to engage in highly speculative investments under a strategy known as *zaitech*, a Japanese word that means, in essence, financial engineering, often through the use of investments unrelated to the company's main business.[42] The strategy worked for a while but by 1990, when the Japanese stock market tanked, Olympus was faced with losses totaling $730 million, which it did not want to disclose to investors. In an attempt to recover the losses, the company began to make even riskier investments using exotic financial instruments. That strategy eventually failed and the firm was sustaining hundreds of millions of dollars in losses every year. But the company's executives were able to hide the losses through a variety of financial sleights of hand, including working with U.S. financial firms like Paine-Webber to move securities losses into offshore vehicles in countries like Bermuda and the Cayman Islands, where they were magically erased from Olympus's balance sheet.[43] In one

[41] Floyd Norris, "Deep Roots of Fraud at Olympus," *New York Times*, December 8, 2001.

[42] In 1986, the president of Olympus told a reporter: "Until last year, I was against *zaitech* but conditions have changed. Somehow we have to make up for this yen strength through non-operating income or our numbers will only worsen. We can no longer dismiss *zaitech* as an evil thing." Nathan Layne, Taro Fuse and James Pomfret, "The Masterminds of the Olympus Coverup," *Reuters*, December 16, 2011, www.reuters.com/article/us-olympus-masterminds-idUSTRE7BF0FB20111216.

[43] *Ibid.*

of these schemes, Olympus used a Singapore banker to set up a special purpose vehicle (SPV) in the British Virgin Islands and then arrange for loans totaling several hundred millions of dollars from his bank to the SPV, collateralized by deposits held by the bank for Olympus. Those funds from those loans were then used to purchase some of the failing investments that Olympus held but wanted to erase from its books. The key to the scheme was the failure by Olympus to disclose to its auditors and shareholders the fact that the loans to the SPV were, in essence, loans from Olympus itself.[44]

These schemes would not have been possible were it not for the assistance of a major international bank, Commerzbank of Germany, which over a period of eleven years transferred $1.6 billion from Olympus into SPVs. Top executives at Commerzbank were apparently unaware of the true purpose of these transactions (i.e., to hide losses from shareholders). Put more accurately, their "non-knowledge" of the purpose could better be described as "willful ignorance." Over the years, a number of Commerzbank employees raised questions about the legality of the Olympus SPVs, but those concerns were dismissed by the bank's upper management. In 2008, a Commerzebank employee in Singapore warned that the transactions were "complex" and "extraordinarily elaborate and redolent of layering [a classic element of money laundering]" and that they "raised suspicions of money laundering, fraud, asset stripping, market manipulation, and derivative Tax offences."[45] Another bank employee warned that if the Olympus deals became public the bank might suffer the way that other scandal-tainted banks had. In an email to his boss he asked: "How will the Board or your boss react to this if any negative news is splash[sic] on the front page news with involvement of Commerzbank?" His boss responded by stating that his email was "dishonorable."[46] No action was

[44] *United States v. Chang Ming Fon*, Case No. S1 13 Cr. 52 (S.D.N.Y. 2011) ("Information"). Olympus Corporation, The Third Party Committee, "Investigation Report Summary" (2011), 22, www.olympus-global.com/en/common/pdf/if111206corpe_2.pd.

[45] New York State Department of Financial Services, *In re Commerzbank AG, Commerzbank, New York Branch* ("Consent Order"), 8.

[46] *United States v. Commerzbank AG, Commerzbank, New York Branch*, Case No. 1:13-cv-08095 (S.D.N.Y. 2013) ("Deferred Prosecution Agreement. Statement of Facts"), 20–21.

taken. The reason for Commerzbank's inaction is clear. Between 2005 and 2010, the bank earned $3 million in fees for its work for Olympus.[47] Yet, this focus on immediate gains may have been shortsighted. In 2015, Commerzbank agreed to pay U.S. authorities $1.5 billion, in part because of its involvement in the Olympus scheme.[48]

The scheme worked for a while, given Japan's relatively lenient accounting rules, but by the mid-2000s, following the debacle at Enron, those rules were changing to make it much more difficult for corporations to hide their losses in offshore entities.[49] Olympus was therefore forced to rely on other means for disguising its losses. The strategy it hit upon involved buying small, money-losing companies at exorbitant prices, writing off the ensuing losses, while recycling the purchase funds and enormous "advisory fees" paid to third parties back to Olympus where they were used to cover the losses incurred by their speculative, zaitech, investments. These schemes were accomplished through a murky web of financial intermediaries and, according to some observers, organized crime (Yakuza) groups.

The illegal accounting scams might have gone unnoticed had it not been for a whistleblower inside Olympus who told what he knew to a small Japanese business magazine. In the summer of 2011 the magazine published a series of articles which questioned why the firm had purchased three unknown, money-losing companies, whose businesses—one was a medical waste recycler, another made facial creams, and the third made plastic containers—had nothing to do with the firm's expertise in manufacturing cameras and medical devices, for a sum of $777 million, far more than the companies' combined market value. The same article pointed to an even more suspicious acquisition made by Olympus in 2007 when it paid $2.2 billion for a British medical device maker (considerably more than what industry analysts thought it was worth), and, even more curious, a total of $687 million in fees to financial intermediaries who

---

[47] Ibid., 27.
[48] Ben Protess, "Commerzbank of Germany to Pay $1.5 Billion in U.S. Case," *New York Times*, March 12, 2015.
[49] Norris, "Deep Roots."

allegedly helped to broker the deal. These fees amounted to 31% of the purchase price where the industry norm would have been closer to 1%.[50]

Even the magazine articles might not have been enough to a trigger a public outcry had it not been for a British national, Michael Woodford, who was recently promoted to CEO of the company, one of the few non-Japanese ever to run a major Japanese corporation. After reading the articles, he confronted the firm's top management and was told not to worry, that it was a minor issue. When he continued to press the matter he was fired and was expected to leave the company quietly.[51] Instead, interest in the case among the foreign media increased dramatically and soon the company was forced to reverse its position as its reputation began to erode.

On November 8, 2011, spokespersons for the Olympus Corporation acknowledged publicly that the company had been deceiving investors and shareholders for years and announced it was commissioning an independent committee to investigate the matter. That panel's report described in detail the schemes by which Olympus hid over $1.5 billion in losses over a period of nearly two decades. The report focused on the corporate culture of Olympus as a main source of the problem; a culture that emphasized loyalty, secrecy, and obedience over ethical standards. "The core part of the management was rotten, and that contaminated other parts around it," the panel wrote. Referring to the deference that characterizes many Japanese managers, "The situation was an epitome of the salaryman mentality in a bad sense."[52]

In many ways the Olympus scandal shared many of the same features found in the Enron debacle: losses hidden in SPVs, accounting gimmicks that made the company look healthier than it was, and compliant accounting firms that assisted in covering up losses. But there were also significant differences. At Enron, top executives reaped huge monetary gains from their illegal schemes. At Olympus, the executives who orchestrated the

---

[50] Michael Woodford, *Exposure* (New York: Portfolio, 2014), 8–11; Tabuchi, "Olympus Hid."

[51] Woodford, *Exposure.*

[52] Kana Inagaki and Phred Dvorak, "Panel Slams Olympus in Accounting Scandal," *Wall Street Journal*, December 6, 2011.

loss cover-up schemes were certainly well paid but there was no comparison with the Enron executives' compensation and there was no suggestion that they personally profited from their misconduct. The Olympus crimes seemed to have been motivated not so much by greed but by what Stanton Wheeler refers to as "fear of falling"—losing status or respect in their professional or personal lives.[53] The accounting frauds were in some ways less about money than they were about face saving among top executives. For example, in one component of the scheme to purchase three money-losing companies and use them to hide losses, Olympus had to pay out more money than the total value of the losses it was trying to conceal. In other words, from a purely economic point of view, it would have been cheaper to just admit the losses, but such an admission would have done serious damage to the corporation's reputation and the reputations of its executives.[54]

DISCUSSION

The companies discussed in this chapter were located in various countries, had very different histories, and were involved in distinct industries. This highlights the fact that corporate accounting fraud can occur in widely varying social and organizational environments.

As discussed in Chapter 1, an important criminological perspective on the sources of corporate crime focuses on *criminogenic markets* and *criminogenic industries* where the structural conditions within those markets and industries are both conducive to and facilitate illegal practices. Researchers have argued that while this perspective has yielded important insights, by focusing on *intra-market* and *intra-industry* conditions, it may also be limited in explaining sophisticated frauds that emerged in the New Economy of the late 1990s and early 2000s, as exemplified by

[53] Stanton Wheeler, "The Problem of White-Collar Crime Motivation," in *White-Collar Crime Reconsidered*, eds. K. Schlegel and D. Weisburd (Boston: Northeastern University Press, 1992): 108–123.

[54] For a detailed discussion of corporate crime and Japanese cases, see Henry N. Pontell and Gilbert Geis, "Black Mist and White Collars: Economic Crime in the U.S. and Japan," *Asian Journal of Criminology* 2(2) (2007): 111–126.

the complex schemes at Enron. Tillman and Indergaard have offered a broader perspective to account for these new business crimes that utilizes the concept of *criminogenic institutional frameworks*, which "refers to the realm of culture and politics involved in the making and enforcement of various kinds of rules"[55] From this perspective complex corporate frauds are not simply related to the particular conditions within industries but are embedded in larger political and cultural arrangements that surround those industries and their actors, and that provide them with the means to fundamentally change the rules governing corporate behavior and, as a result, "normalize" what would more widely be considered illegal behavior. In applying this perspective to the New Economy scandals of the early 2000s they argued that those scandals.

> . . . resulted from the intersection of rules nested at three levels of corporate governance: 1) Congress under the influence of corporate contributors and free market ideologies, set the general tone by promoting "market" rules while gutting protections for ordinary investors; 2) business professionals who were supposed to monitor corporations, cashed in on their positions of institutionalized trust by joining executives in propagating New Economy Business rules in particular sectors; and 3) small circles that controlled access to the "deal flow" in effect, made their own rules as they developed norms and routines that helped organize (and normalize) collective corruption.[56]

The corrupt practices that became institutionalized at Enron continued for so long and were so well-hidden because executives at the firm "systematically changed the economic rules" by building "an elaborate network of interlocking connections to politicians, regulators, bankers, accountants, public relations experts, and media heads."[57]

---

[55] Robert Tillman and Michael Indergaard, "Corporate Corruption in the New Economy," in *International Handbook of White-Collar and Corporate Crime*, eds. Henry Pontell and Gilbert Geis (New York: Springer, 2007): 474–489.

[56] *Ibid.*

[57] Tillman and Indergaard, *Pump and Dump*, 76.

In the cases analyzed here we see the importance of these linkages to organizations and individuals outside the companies and their industries. First, in all three cases corporate executives were aided and abetted in their cover-ups by prestigious accounting firms. They were among the "business professionals who were supposed to monitor corporations" but who instead became colluders with their clients in schemes to defraud investors and regulators. At Enron, it was primarily Arthur Andersen that took on this role. At Satyam, it was Price Waterhouse Coopers. At Olympus, it was Arthur Andersen, KPMG, and later Ernst & Young. The clean bills of health provided by these firms helped to shield the companies from regulatory scrutiny by delaying full investigations.

Another common feature of these cases presented here is the role played by a compliant media. The business media, in particular, often served as "cheerleaders" for the firms as they rose to the top of their industries, shielding them and their executives from critical scrutiny, despite the presence of warning signs. And, even after suspicions were raised, the media often failed to give adequate attention to the cases or downplayed their significance. For example, after the journalist Yamaguchi Yoshimasa published the initial article for a small business magazine that raised questions about Olympus's acquisition of three companies at inflated prices, he tried to persuade larger Japanese magazines to publish his follow-up stories on what appeared to be a major corporate scandal. To his surprise, "my proposals were ignored. In most cases, the magazines did not even bother to return my calls."[58] Similarly, in September 2000, over a year before Enron began to collapse and six months before any other journalists began to question Enron's success, Johnathan Weil wrote a story in a regional supplement to the *Wall Street Journal* in which he raised critical questions about how Enron and other energy companies were manipulating their balance sheets to show profits rather than losses. But the story received almost no attention from the business press and Wall Street analysts continued to rate Enron a "strong buy."[59] In a rare act of contrition,

[58] Yamaguchi Yoshimasa "Olympus Scandal Exposes the Shortcomings of the Japanese Media," *Nippon.com*, January 16, 2012, www.nippon.com/en/currents/d00013/.

[59] Tillman and Indergaard, *Pump and Dump*, 86.

Business Week later admitted that the magazine, along with the press in general, had failed to ask critical questions about Enron until it was too late. Instead, "the press blithely accepted Enron as the epitome of a new, post-deregulation corporate model when it should have been much more aggressive in probing the company's opaque partnerships, off balance sheet maneuvers, and soaring leverage."[60]

The companies' illegal practices were also masked by sympathetic (or at least incurious) regulators who took their cues from powerful politicians, links to whom were carefully cultivated by corporate executives. At Enron, the close ties between the CEO Kenneth Lay and George W. Bush (both when he was President and when he was governor of Texas) were well-known. The links between business and government in Japan are so close that the country is often referred to as "Japan, Inc." But the ties between Olympus executives and politicians were particularly close, a relationship that continued even after the scandal subsided. Three former top executives of the firm were eventually convicted on charges related to the fraud but all received suspended sentences despite overwhelming evidence of their guilt and the scope of their illegal behavior.[61] In India, Ramalinga Raju, the head of Satyam, was particularly close to the Chief Minister of Andhra Pradesh (the equivalent of a U.S. governor) in Hyderabad—so much so that when President Bill Clinton visited the area in 2000, Raju was seated next to him on the podium.[62]

If one steps away from the thicket of details in these complicated cases a more fundamental perspective on accounting fraud, as a form of financial crime, emerges. All three companies followed the logic of financialization to pursue investments outside their original products and services and to seek profits in risky, speculative ventures. When these ventures went sour and the companies started to show significant losses, the executives concocted schemes to hide the losses from investors and regulators. Like Ponzi schemes, these cover-ups can only be successful for so long,

[60] "Enron: Let Us Count the Culprits," *Business Week*, December 17, 2001,154; Bethany McLean and Peter Elkind, *The Smartest Guys in the Room* (New York: Penguin, 2004).

[61] "Olympus scandal: Former executives sentenced," BBC News, July 3, 2013, www.bbc .com/news/business-23156879.

[62] Bhupesh Bhandari, *The Satyam Saga* (New Delhi: Business Standard Books, 2009), 92.

and they are eventually uncovered leading to familiar allegations of corporate abuse and vows by government officials to prevent similar scandals in the future.

Cases of high-level corporate accounting fraud also reveal a fundamental hypocrisy common in the contemporary corporate world. While many of these companies' executives are ardent exponents of "free markets"— operating relatively unfettered by government regulation or burdensome taxes—they also spend much of their time attempting to avoid the penalties those markets can impose on their participants when they fail to perform. Kenneth Lay, the former CEO of Enron who was eventually convicted on felony charges, for example, was a loud and shrill critic of government and a promoter of deregulation. Yet, the accounting schemes that were undertaken on his watch, in which hundreds of millions dollars in losses were hidden, were nothing if not an attempt to deny market participants, like the pension funds that invested heavily in Enron's stock, access to critical information about the company's actual performance. Even in the wake of the Enron scandal, prominent members of the business community as well as academics continued to support the company's "innovations." As two prominent business school professors put it: "[W]e must be careful not to indict everything the firm did . . . the firm moved entrepreneurially into new areas and put itself to the test of the market. Without that spirit of innovation, the process of capitalism would grind to a halt."[63] In light of what we now know about Enron's extensive efforts to falsely portray itself, the argument that the company put itself to the "test of the market" could only be seen (by most reasonable observers) as patently absurd.

---

[63] Christopher Culp and Steve Hanke, "Empire of the Sun: An Economic Interpretation of Enron's Energy Business," *Policy Analysis* no. 470 (2003): 17.

[4]

DEALING WITH THE
DISREPUTABLE

Corporations are fundamentally amoral, according to some theorists,[1] which means that their primary, legally mandated goal is to pursue profits irrespective of the moral consequences of their actions.[2] As a result corporate actors are reluctant to recognize the essentially moral distinctions made by governments between good and bad, or reputable and disreputable, business partners and clients. Financial institutions in particular desire to be free to do business with whomever they wish. But this can also cause them to run afoul of numerous sovereign laws that restrict financial transactions with persons and entities deemed to be engaged in illegal, harmful or threatening activities.

This conflict results in two fundamental forms of financial crime: money laundering and violations of laws (Office of Foreign Assets Control (OFAC) laws) that restrict transactions with certain countries and individuals. In this chapter we focus on case studies of money laundering and consider why seemingly reputable institutions would be drawn to this illegal practice.

A fundamental problem for individuals involved in illegal enterprises is how to use their ill-gotten gains in the legitimate economy without attracting the attention of law enforcement agencies. Many of these enterprises involve cash-only transactions (drug dealers generally do not take

---

[1] Joel Balkan, *The Corporation: The Pathological Pursuit of Profit and Power* (New York: Free Press, 2004).

[2] Milton Friedman, "The Social Responsibility of Business is to Increase Its Profits," *New York Times Magazine*, September 13, 1970.

credit cards), so a successful criminal who pulls off a crime is still faced with the problem of how to convert this cash into something more fungible. If they cannot do this, or gain access to the proceeds of their crimes, then their risks are pointless. But even if the transactions do not involve cash, there is still a need to disguise the source and ownership of the funds to put them to use in the legitimate economy.

To illustrate, consider a simple case. In the 1980s, Stew Leonard ran a chain of very successful grocery stores bearing his name in Connecticut. Leonard and his stores, where the corporate slogan was "the customer is always right," were frequently praised in the business media for their innovations in retailing and marketing. It was later discovered that throughout the 1980s Leonard, his son and two brothers-in-law had used a sophisticated computer program to skim over $17 million in cash from the stores, on which they paid no taxes. The problem was that Leonard could not use the cash in any substantial amounts in the United States without drawing the attention of tax authorities. So, Leonard and his associates opened bank accounts on the Caribbean island of St. Martin where Leonard happened to own a home. They bundled up the cash in suitcases or shopping bags which they would take with them on their frequent trips to the island. The beginning of the end of the scheme occurred in the spring of 1991 when customs officials examined Leonard's luggage on a flight to St. Martin's and found $50,000 in undeclared cash.[3] Investigators later discovered the computer program in the stores that generated false records of receipts. In 1993, Leonard was sentenced to fifty-two months in prison.

The problems faced by Leonard are the same problems faced by international criminals, only theirs are more complicated and involve larger sums of money. Since most financial institutions are required to report cash transactions in excess of $10,000 to the Department of Treasury, legitimate financial institutions would seem to be shut off as means to "clean" illicit proceeds from illicit activities. That might be true for low-level drug dealers whose accounts would rarely be very large, but large financial institutions are loath to turn away accounts that total in the

[3] United States v. Leonard & Guthman, 37 F.3d 32 (2d Cir. 1994).

millions of dollars and represent potentially significant revenues from fees and commissions. As we shall see later, many of those institutions have not been able to resist the lure of those lucrative accounts. The United Nations Office on Drugs and Crime has estimated that in 2009 approximately 2.7% of world gross domestic product (GDP), or $1.6 trillion in illicit funds, were laundered worldwide.[4] In the past, money laundering was often a local affair with organized crime members using a variety of cash businesses—laundries, car washes, restaurants—to "clean" their illicit funds. Today most money laundering is done by financial institutions. Colombian economists Daniel Mejia and Alejandro Gaviria estimate, for example, that 97% of the profits from the Colombian cocaine trade leaves that country, with much of it ending up in U.S. and European banks.[5] Recent cases involving money-laundering allegations against major international financial institutions confirm this hypothesis. The pressures and opportunities to process illicit funds within financial institutions, even those with presumably impeccable moral credentials, are illustrated by revelations of money laundering at one of the world's most respected institutions: the Vatican.

MONEY LAUNDERING AND THE HOLY SEE

Geographically, Vatican City is a tiny enclave in the center of Rome. Politically it is an independent sovereign state that is ruled by the Pope and contains its own independent institutions, including its own bank. Until recently, that bank operated under its own set of rules and was overseen by authorities in the Vatican and its records were not available to outsiders. This made it a perfect vehicle for money laundering, and over the years a number of people have alleged that it was used for exactly that purpose. Two recent cases illustrate this point.

[4] United Nations Office on Drugs and Crime, *Estimating Illicit Financial Flows Resulting from Drug Trafficking and Other Transnational Organized Crimes* (Vienna: United Nations Office on Drugs and Crime, 2011), 7.
[5] Ed Vulliamy, "Western Banks Reaping Billions From Colombian Cocaine Trade," *The Guardian*, June 2, 2012.

In the early 1990s, Martin Frankel, a forty-something high school dropout working in the securities industry, conducted a scheme to acquire a number of U.S. insurance companies. He was able to do this despite the fact that in 1992, the SEC permanently barred him from the securities industry for misleading investors. He disguised his ownership of the companies by operating through a trust that he set up, and apparently state insurance regulators never questioned who was behind the trust. He eventually controlled seven insurance companies, located mostly in southern states, from which by 1999 he had looted over $200 million. He used the proceeds to fund a lavish and sometimes bizarre lifestyle that he conducted from his palatial home in Connecticut, where he maintained a "household" of young women, many of whom were imported from foreign countries. These women enjoyed a posh lifestyle that included "theater tickets, international travel . . . a sable coat that was bought and returned to Saks Fifth Avenue, and meals at Jean Georges, one of Manhattan's most exclusive restaurants."[6]

Frankel must have known that his scheme would ultimately unravel and that he would have to flee, so he began setting up a complicated scheme to get himself and his ill-gotten gains out of the country, a scheme that involved the Vatican bank. Using the phony name David Rosse, his first step was to contact a well-connected New York lawyer, Tom Bolan, who had advised President Reagan and New York Senator Alphonse D'Amato, and express his desire to set up a trust fund to be administered through accounts in the Vatican bank to give money to Catholic causes (despite the fact that Frankel was Jewish). Bolan, who had many connections and dealings with the Church, then contacted Father Peter Jacobs who lived in Rome and explained that he was in contact with a wealthy American who wanted to help Catholic organizations. Under the plan Rosse (Frankel) would transfer $55 million to the Vatican bank, which would set up an account under the name "Saint Francis of Assisi Foundation," which would then transfer $50 million to a U.S. brokerage firm account. The remaining

---

[6] Ellen Joan Pollock, Steve Stecklow, Michael Allen, Mitchell Pacelle and Deborah Lohse, "His Days of Dried Peas Over, Frankel Scrambled for Gems, Freedom," *Wall Street Journal*, July 16, 1999.

$5 million would be paid as a fee to the Vatican bank. Not wanting to turn down such a lucrative offer, Vatican officials refrained from asking too many questions, and went through with the plan.[7]

Frankel's scheme began to unravel in 1999, when insurance regulators in Mississippi began questioning the quality of the assets behind one of the companies that Frankel had purchased. In the spring of 1999, Frankel/Rosse and several of his associates were summoned to a meeting in Jackson, Mississippi, with insurance regulators who peppered them with questions about the sources of their funds, for which they had few answers. Frankel returned to Connecticut and immediately began to shut down his operation and prepared to flee the country. In a final attempt to get rid of evidence he even set fire to his $3 million home. But he did not get rid of all the evidence. Investigators would later find a to-do note that Frankel wrote to himself that read: "Launder more money, NOW." Five days later, Frankel boarded a private plane and flew to Rome.[8] From there Frankel went to Germany from where he was eventually extradited back to the United States. In 2002 Frankel was sentenced to seventeen years in prison for his crimes.

The story of Martin Frankel, the con man, is not all that remarkable. Less expected, however, is the involvement of the Vatican bank in this sordid tale. Vatican officials claimed that they were victims as well, who were deceived by Frankel. But the facts in the case point to a complex effort to distance the Holy See from Rosse/Frankel while still collecting the promised millions in "fees." According to an exhaustive *Fortune* magazine investigation, Vatican officials were uncomfortable with having Frankel's charity operating from within the Vatican and required that instead the relationship be mediated by a third entity, the Monitor Ecclesiasticus (ME), a little known organization that operated independently from but had close relationships with the Vatican.[9] The funds would then flow through the ME, and then back to the Saint Francis of Assisi Foundation. In money-laundering terminology, this is known as "layering." The

[7] Richard Behar, "Washing Money in the Holy See," *Fortune*, August 16, 1999.
[8] Lynda Edwards, "Trail of Stolen Money Leads to Rome," *Washington Post*, August 8, 2004.
[9] Behar, "Washing Money."

money was never actually transferred but a structure was put in place that allowed Frankel to use his "immaculate connection" to purchase more insurance companies and loot them.

More recently the Vatican bank has been hit with even more serious allegations of financial fraud. In June2013, a Vatican official and two others were arrested and charged with conspiring to transport $26 million out of Switzerland and into Italy aboard a private jet. At the center of the scheme, which was never carried out, was Msgr. Nunzio Scarano, a top accountant at the Vatican office that managed real estate investments for the Holy See. The plot was complicated but involved an attempt by Msgr. Scarano to repatriate money to Vatican accounts to cover losses incurred by individuals whom had invested funds with a friend of Scarano's, Giovanni Carenzio, in what prosecutors would call a Ponzi scheme. Many of the investors were friends of Scarano's who had invested because he had vouched for Carenzio's trustworthiness.[10] When investigators looked into Msgr. Scarano's personal finances they discovered that he lived in a seventeen-room, $17.5 million house and had assets of $8.2 million, all on an annual salary of $41,000 from the Vatican.[11] His lifestyle was consistent with his nickname, *Don cinquecento* (Monsignor 500) because "he habitually flashed a thick wad of cash and boasted that the 500-euro note ($670) was his favorite."[12]

As of this writing Scarano is facing a potential sentence of twenty years in prison. After the monsignor's arrest the Vatican bank officials "discovered" over 100 suspicious transaction worth hundreds of millions of euros. The bank could not fully account for the money's origins but one Vatican official took an "all's well that ends well" position: stating: "it is all the Vatican's money, anyway...."[13]

This scandal was just one of many that the Vatican has faced in recent decades. Again, the actions of a rogue priest are not as important, for our

---

[10] David Casati, "Of Virtue and Vice, and a Vatican Priest," *New York Times*, October 18, 2014.

[11] *Ibid.*

[12] Gerald Posner, *God's Bankers*, (New York: Simon and Schuster, 2015), 505.

[13] Gaia Pianigianidec,"Vatican Finds Stash of Money 'Tucked Away,'" *New York Times*, December 4, 2014.

purposes, as the conditions within and surrounding the Vatican that has made it so vulnerable to financial crime. For decades the bank had operated as a means for managing the Holy See's internal accounts. But by the late twentieth century it had become a tax haven for wealthy Italians seeking to hide their money from the tax man and for corrupt politicians attempting to disguise the sources of their funds. The Vatican bank has been particularly vulnerable to money laundering because of the historical secrecy in which its operations have been conducted. No outside regulatory agency, until recently, went over its books and raised questions about its customers and the sources of their deposits. Despite pledges to become more transparent and open, in 2012 the Holy See found itself on a list compiled by the U.S. State Department of sixty-eight countries or jurisdictions that were "of concern" for possible money-laundering activities.[14]

The Vatican bank may be seen as a special case, but even at large, "reputable" international banks, which are relatively highly regulated, whose operations are routinely scrutinized by outside authorities, one can find large-scale, rampant money-laundering activities. Recent scandals at several major banks have brought the point home that not only does laundering transpire in the dark recesses of the criminal underworld, but it can take place virtually in the open at well-known and well-respected financial institutions.

BIG BANKS AND BAD MONEY

On April 10, 2006, Mexican soldiers boarded a DC-9 jet that had landed at the international airport in Ciudad del Carmen. Once onboard, the soldiers discovered 128 black suitcases containing 5.7 tons of cocaine, with a street value of $100 million. Even by the standards of Mexican drug dealers this was a pretty big haul. But when investigators began to look into the provenance of the plane itself they found something even more interesting. The plane had been purchased in Florida by cocaine

[14] Nicole Winfield, "Vatican Tries to Explain U.S. Classification as Potential Money Laundering Hub," *Huffington Post*, March 3, 2012, www.huffingtonpost.com/2012/03/10/vatican-money-laundering_n_1336650.html.

smugglers working out of Mexico using accounts at Wachovia Bank in Miami.[15] At the time, Wachovia was the sixth largest bank in the United States, with assets of over $700 billion. The funds in those accounts had been transferred from *casas de cambio* (CDCs) in Mexico. CDCs are not actually banks but are currency exchange businesses that allow an individual in Mexico to exchange pesos for dollars and then wire the dollars to accounts in the United States. "A central function of CDCs is to allow persons or businesses in Mexico to exchange or wire transfer the value of hard currency from Mexico to bank accounts in the U.S. or other countries to conduct commerce."[16]

When U.S. investigators examined Wachovia accounts held by Mexican CDCs they saw evidence of extensive money-laundering activities. They found, for example, that between 2004 and 2007 $13 million passed through these accounts which was used to purchase four airplanes used by drug smugglers that were eventually seized by foreign law enforcement agencies and which were found to contain a total of 20,000 kilograms of cocaine.[17] To get a sense of scale, using the United Nations estimate that the average cocaine user in the United States consumes 31 kilograms of cocaine a year, we can calculate that those 20,000 kilograms would have kept 645,161 Americans supplied with cocaine for a year.[18]

During this period, the early 2000s, Mexican CDCs were under increased scrutiny as the source of illicit funds into the United States.[19] Despite this growing concern, between 2004 and 2007 Wachovia processed $373 billion in wire transfers from CDCs.[20] Investigators were able to identify accounts containing $110 million in drug money, the sources of which

[15] Michael Smith, "Banks Financing Mexico Drug Gangs Admitted in Wells Fargo Deal," *Bloomberg News,* June 29, 2010.

[16] *United States v. Wachovia Bank, N.A.*, Case No.: 10-20165 (SDFL 2010) ("Factual Statement"), 3.

[17] *Ibid.*

[18] United Nations Office on Drugs and Crime. *The Globalization of Crime* (Vienna: United Nations Office on Drugs and Crime, 2010), 89.

[19] "The Role of U.S. Correspondent Banking in International Money Laundering," Hearings before the Senate Comm. on Governmental Affairs, Permanent Subcomm. on Investigations, 107th Cong. (2001).

[20] *United States v. Wachovia*, 5.

Wachovia claimed to be unaware.[21] The U.S. Attorney who prosecuted the case stated: "Wachovia's blatant disregard for our banking laws gave international cocaine cartels a virtual carte blanche to finance their operations."[22]

Despite obvious red flags indicating suspicious transactions in its own bank and as other banks departed the market following warnings from federal officials about potential money-laundering potential, during the mid-2000s, Wachovia sought to expand its CDC business. When its own anti-money-laundering expert, a former police official in Britain, warned bank officials that many of the transactions with foreign CDCs looked suspicious he was told he had no right to look at foreign transactions and that he should cease filing suspicious activity reports.[23] At the time, the bank was losing billions of dollars from its exposure to subprime mortgage loans; by 2008 those losses totaled $26 billion.[24] Some observers have suggested that the declining profits at the bank pushed executives to desperately seek new business without asking too many questions about their new clients.

On March 12, 2010, federal prosecutors finally took action, filing a sealed, criminal information charging the bank with failing to maintain an adequate anti-laundering program. Just five days later prosecutors announced that they had reached a deferred prosecution agreement with the bank. As part of the agreement the bank agreed to pay $110 million in civil penalties and $50 million in fines. In return, if the bank complied with certain restrictions, in 12 months the criminal charges would be dropped.[25] No single individual at Wachovia was ever charged with a crime, despite massive evidence that many at the bank knew what was going on with the drug dealer transactions. The media reaction to the settlement was swift, with most commentators critically citing it as an example of a "too big to jail" policy in which the big players, executives, and the banks themselves rarely face criminal sanctions even when they are caught red-handed

[21] *Ibid.*, 6.

[22] Smith, "Banks Financing. . . ."

[23] Ed Vulliamy, "The Wachovia Whistleblower," *The Nation*, December 9, 2010, www .thenation.com/article/wachovia-whistleblower/.

[24] Smith, "Banks Financing . . . ."

[25] U.S. Attorney's Office, Southern District of Florida, "Wachovia Enters into Deferred Prosecution Agreement," news release, March 17, 2010, www.justice.gov/archive/usao/ fls/PressReleases/2010/100317-02.html.

working closely with well-known criminals and violating U.S. laws, leaving only lower-level criminals to be the symbolic targets of tough law enforcement efforts. But the howls of public outrage over the lenient treatment of banks caught colluding with drug cartels and organized crime groups would grow louder two years later.

On July 17, 2012, the U.S. Senate Permanent Subcommittee on Investigations released a blistering, 335-page report detailing numerous violations of U.S. laws at HSBC, one of the largest banks in the world. The scope and duration of the illegal activity was stunning. As the chair of the Subcommittee, Carl Levin, put it:

> HSBC used its U.S. bank as a gateway into the U.S. financial system for some HSBC affiliates around the world to provide U.S. dollar services to clients while playing fast and loose with U.S. banking rules. Due to poor AML [anti-money laundering] controls, HBUS exposed the United States to Mexican drug money, suspicious travelers cheques, bearer share corporations, and rogue jurisdictions.[26]

Not only did the committee point to crimes within the bank, but it was also highly critical of American bank regulators, particularly the Office of the Comptroller of the Currency (OCC), claiming that the agency was aware of the money-laundering activity at HSBC but tolerated the problems for five years without taking any action.[27]

HSBC is a large, complex, international financial institution. As of 2012, it held $2.5 trillion in assets, had 89 million customers, and employed some 300,000 people.[28] Headquartered in London, it operated in

---

[26] U.S Senate, Permanent Subcomm. on Investigations, "HSBC Exposed U.S. Financial System to Money Laundering, Drug, Terrorist Financing Risk," news release, July 16, 2012, www.hsgac.senate.gov/subcommittees/investigations/media/hsbc-exposed-us-finacial-system-to-money-laundering-drug-terrorist financing-risks.

[27] *U.S. Vulnerabilities to Money Laundering, Drugs, and Terrorist Financing: HSBC Case History, V. 1,* Senate Comm. on Homeland Security and Governmental Affairs, Permanent Subcomm. on Investigations, 112th Cong. 6 (2012), 6.

[28] Senate Comm. on Homeland Security and Governmental Affairs, Permanent Subcomm. on Investigations, *U.S. Vulnerabilities to Money Laundering, Drugs, and Terrorist Financing: HSBC Case History,* S. Rep. (2002), 2.

eighty countries. In the United States its business is conducted primarily by HSBC Bank U.S.A. N.A. (known as "H-BUS"). H-BUS was designed to serve as a gateway for foreign money into U.S. financial markets. This is accomplished through foreign affiliates that have access to what are known as correspondent accounts at U.S. branches of H-BUS. Correspondent banking has a history of serving as a money-laundering mechanism by allowing funds in foreign accounts to be converted to U.S. dollars and then moved into other parts of the U.S. financial system.[29]

In the late 1990s and 2000s, the illicit narcotics industry, particularly the cocaine business, shifted from its base in Colombia to Mexico and the industry leaders were increasingly Mexican organized crime groups rather than Colombian drug cartels. In 2012, the State Department estimated that "drug cartels were using Mexican and U.S. financial institutions to launder as much as $39 billion each year."[30] By the mid-2000s American authorities were aware of threat posed by Mexican drug money launderers, particularly through correspondent banking, and began to inform banks of the need to scrutinize carefully the movement of cash out of Mexico and into U.S. accounts. Most U.S. banks complied and began cracking down on suspicious transactions involving Mexican institutions and accounts held by Mexican citizens. As a result:

> . . . [b]ecause drug traffickers in the United States were having difficulty finding a U.S. financial institution that would accept large amounts of cash, due to strict U.S. AML [anti-money laundering] controls, many were instead transporting large volumes of U.S. dollars to Mexico, and depositing the dollars at Mexican financial institutions. The drug traffickers could then keep their deposits in U.S. dollars through the Mexican financial institution's correspondent account at a U.S. bank, or exchange the dollars for pesos.[31]

---

[29] Permanent Subcommittee, "Role of U.S. Correspondent Banking."
[30] Permanent Subcommittee, *U.S. Vulnerabilities*, S. Rep., 40.
[31] *Ibid.*, 45.

One method used by drug dealers to move the cash was to go through HSBC's Mexican affiliate, HBMX. Between 2007 and 2008, HBMX transferred $7 billion to accounts at HSBC, far more than any other affiliate. Law enforcement agencies in both the United States and Mexico concluded that the only way that much money could be transferred was if it included significant amounts of cash from drug cartels.[32]

Many of HBMX's activities were highly suspicious. One of the more glaring red flags was the fact that HBMX operated a branch in the Cayman Islands that, by 2008, despite having no physical presence in the islands, had 50,000 clients with $2.1 billion in assets. The total population of the Cayman Islands is less than 60,000 so, obviously, most of these accounts were held by foreigners. Moreover, for many of these accounts the bank had little or no information about the account holders, making it possible for drug cartels to transfer large amounts of cash with no questions asked. In 2008, HSBC officials grudgingly acknowledged that maybe some of the account holders in the Cayman Islands were a bit shady and began closing accounts. But by 2012, the branch still had 20,000 accounts.[33]

Another highly suspicious type of transaction conducted by HBMX involved traveler's checks. This form of payment is familiar to many who have purchased them to use when traveling on vacations, particularly in foreign countries. They can be issued in many currencies and have serial numbers that record information about the purchaser so that they can be replaced if lost or stolen. Law enforcement agencies have long warned about the potential for these financial instruments to be used to launder cash generated by illicit activities. HBMX sold large volumes of traveler's checks. In one quarter of 2004, the bank sold over $10 million worth of the checks—one-third of the total amount sold by the bank as a whole. Why, one might ask, would Mexicans need so many traveler's checks? Average Mexican citizens did not, but organized crime groups did. The bank made it easy for individuals

[32] Ibid., 36.
[33] Ibid., 99.

to purchase large amounts of checks with no questions asked, allowing those clients deemed to be non-suspicious to purchase as much as $250,000 worth of travelers checks at a time (very expensive vacations indeed).[34]

The Permanent Subcommittee turned up evidence that many of these purchases were being made to launder drug money. In one case, over a seven-month period, 1,500 traveler's checks, with a combined value of $900,000 were purchased at the same HBMX branch and later cashed at car auctions in the United States.

Another HBMX branch sold traveler's checks to the same two men over a period of three years, with a total value of $1.9 million. When buying the checks the men signed with illegible signatures so that their identities could not be traced.[35]

A legitimate part of the financial system involves the transfer of cash from one geographical location to another. HBSC was one of a number of institutions that would buy and sell currencies in bulk from institutions in other countries. Between 2006 and 2008, HSBC's U.S. subsidiary H-BUS received $15 billion in bulk cash transfers from HSBC affiliates around the world. A disproportionate amount of transfers came from Mexico. In the two-year period from 2006 to 2007, HBMX sent $7 billion in cash to H-BUS, far more than any other Mexican bank—even those much larger than HBMX. Regulators warned that such large shipments of cash undoubtedly included significant amounts of drug money. According to the U.S. Department of Justice, "from 2006 to 2010, the Sinaloa Cartel in Mexico, the Norte del Valle Cartel in Colombia, and other drug traffickers laundered at least $881 million in illegal narcotics trafficking proceeds through HSBC Bank USA."[36] The Sinaloa Cartel, headed by the murderous Chapo Guzman, was a particularly violent organization responsible for the deaths of hundreds of Mexicans. The volumes of cash were so large that the drug dealers discovered that the boxes of cash they delivered to

[34] *Ibid.*, 100–102.

[35] *Ibid.*, 103.

[36] U.S. Department of Justice, "Assistant Attorney General Lanny A. Breuer Speaks at the HSBC Press Conference," news release, December 11, 2012, www.justice.gov/opa/speech/assistant-attorney-general-lanny-breuer-speaks-hsbc-press-conference.

Mexican banks were too large to fit through tellers' windows and so had to design boxes with precise dimensions. The Justice Department also claimed that between 2006 and 2009, H-BUS failed to monitor over $9.4 billion in bulk cash purchases from HBMX.[37]

The Permanent Subcommittee's investigation turned up internal documents from HSBC that revealed the banality of corporate crime among those who are involved. In January 2008, the Sigue Corporation, a U.S. money servicing company whose principal business involved wiring remittances from the United States to Mexico, entered into a deferred prosecution agreement after prosecutors alleged that the company had "allowed tens of millions of dollars of suspicious financial transactions to be conducted through Sigue, including funds represented by undercover U.S. law enforcement agents to be drug proceeds."[38] Despite this admission of guilt, H-BUS decided to retain Sigue as a client of HBMX, with one executive explaining in an email that "the events for which [Sigue] have been fined were relatively historic—from memory, 2–3 years ago, and significant improvements had been made since then." Another executive wrote that Sigue "had little control over its numerous agents" and noted that "Whilst the company will now need to take steps to address these deficiencies this will inevitably take some time, and instilling the appropriate culture within the business even longer."[39] Thus, even after one of its major clients was revealed to be deeply involved in laundering drug money H-BUS decided to continue doing business with the firm, rationalizing that decision with thin excuses for its prior misconduct.

Another notorious client of HBMX was Casia de Cambio Puebla (Puebla). Puebla was at the center of the Wachovia scandal and in 2007 U.S. authorities seized $11 million in accounts held by Puebla at Wachovia. Puebla was an important customer for HBMX as well, increasing its purchases of U.S. dollars from $18 million in 2005 to $113 million in 2007. This increase in volume alone should have alerted H-BUS officials

[37] *Ibid.*
[38] Permanent Subcommittee on Investigations, *U.S. Vulnerabilities*, S. Rep., 85.
[39] *Ibid.*, 87.

to the possibility of money laundering. Instead, officials at the bank offered a number of weak explanations for the increase. One HBUS banker
wrote: "[c]lient is slowing [sic] growing its business volume as a result of
better cash flow thanks to dealing with HSBC i.e., faster turnaround of
banknotes." The same banker later offered this explanation for the sudden
increase in business: "There is [a] large population of Mexican[s] working
in the U.S. during the summer months (landscaping) that send money
back home (religiously) to their families."[40] This theory might be true in
general but would not explain why Puebla's remittances to Mexico from
the United States increased from $27 million one year to $50 million the
next year with no corresponding increase in the number of Mexican workers in the United States. This was a convenient explanation that allowed
the bankers at H-BUS to ignore the obvious, that one of their clients was
using its services to launder illegal proceeds.

One might think that with such damning evidence of widespread criminal misconduct indictments would have rained down on HSBC employees. Instead, at a press conference on December 11, 2012, Assistant Attorney General Lanny Breuer, after stating that the bank had "permit[ed]
narcotics traffickers and others to launder hundreds of millions of dollars
through HSBC subsidiaries," announced that the Justice Department had
entered into a deferred prosecution agreement with HSBC in which the
bank and its employees would face *no criminal prosecution* in exchange
for paying fines, penalties, and forfeitures totaling over $1.9 billion.[41]
After the deal was announced HSBC's CEO (chief executive officer) was
slightly contrite, stating, "We accept responsibility for our past mistakes.
We have said we are profoundly sorry for them."[42] And, just to show how
serious he was, he announced that the bank would "partially defer bonus
compensation for its most senior officials during the five-year period of
the deferred prosecution agreement."[43] In other words, "a penalty " for
supporting the operations of drug moguls who were responsible for the

[40] *Ibid.*, 84.
[41] U.S. Department of Justice, "Assistant Attorney General Lanny A. Breuer Speaks."
[42] Ed Vulliamy, "HSBC Has Form: Remember Mexico and Laundered Drug Money," *The Guardian*, February 15, 2005.
[43] *Ibid.*

deaths of thousands of individuals, was that top executives at HSBC would be paid somewhat less extravagantly.

The response to the announced deal was immediate and harsh, with commentators denouncing the agreement as an outrageous, flagrant display of the lenient treatment afforded corporate criminals. *Rolling Stone* journalist Matt Taibbi captured the widespread outrage when he wrote: "Yes, they issued a fine–$1.9 billion, or about five weeks' profit–but they didn't extract so much as one dollar or one day in jail from any individual, despite a decade of stupefying abuses."[44] There was considerable speculation in the media about what lay behind the decision not to prosecute HSBC. One of these was the "too big to jail" argument which held that prosecutors feared the consequences that prosecuting a very large financial institution might have for the economy.

Considerable weight was added to this explanation in July 2016 when House Republicans released a report, aptly titled *Too Big to Jail*, which examined the process by which the decision was made inside the Department of Justice (DOJ) not to prosecute HSBC or any of its employees. According to the report, prosecutors in DOJ's money-laundering unit had originally recommended seeking a guilty plea from HSBC, but was ultimately overruled by senior DOJ leadership who were concerned that "prosecuting the bank would have serious adverse consequences on the financial system."[45] One of the factors that influenced this decision was a letter from Britain's chief finance minister, George Osborne, to the chairman of the Federal Reserve in which he "insinuated . . . that the U.S. was unfairly targeting U.K. banks" and that prosecuting HSBC "could lead to [financial] contagion" and pose "very serious implications for financial and economic stability, particularly in Europe and Asia."[46] These findings contradicted former Attorney General Eric Holder's earlier statement that "banks are not too big to jail."[47] The House report's findings would also seem to affirm the point made by Calavita, Pontell, and Tillman

---

[44] Matt Taibbi, "Gangster Banksters," *Rolling Stone*, February 14, 2013.

[45] House Committee on Financial Services, *Too Big to Jail: Inside the Obama Justice Department's Decision not to Hold Wall Street Accountable*, H. Rep. (2016), 12.

[46] *Ibid.*, 14.

[47] *Ibid.*, 11.

that in cases involving financial institutions the state's primary interest is not in crime control—the pursuit of individual or corporate criminal offenders—but rather in "damage control," stabilizing the economy.[48]

It might be tempting to see the Wachovia and HSBC cases as anomalies within the larger banking world, but it is important to understand that these were not the first instances in which a major U.S financial institution was caught laundering money for Mexican drug dealers. In the late 1990s, New York-based Citibank was accused by a senate committee of helping Raul Salinas, the brother of the former president of Mexico, move $100 million out of Mexico and into Swiss bank accounts. Salinas allegedly made the money by using his political influence to help drug cartels ship cocaine from Mexico into the United States. Bankers at Citibank arranged for a complicated series of transfers in which the money first went to a Mexican branch of the bank, then to accounts in New York, then to accounts in London and Switzerland, from where the money was invested for Mr. Salinas. Citibank representatives would later claim that they thought

> . . . . all of Mr. Salinas's funds had been obtained legally, with a large proportion resulting from the sale of a construction company that he owned. However, Citibank knew no details about the construction company, its name, who had purchased it, or the amount of money generated by sale.[49]

Perhaps their "see no evil" attitude was influenced by the fact that Citibank earned $1.1 million for handling Mr. Salinas's money. In 1995, with his brother out of office and his political cover gone, Raul Salinas was arrested for killing a rival, for which he was eventually sentenced to 50 years in prison. Neither Citibank itself nor any of its employees were ever charged with a crime.

---

[48] Kitty Calavita, Henry Pontell and Robert Tillman, *Big Money Crime* (Berkeley: University of California Press, 1997), 136.

[49] General Accounting Office, *Private Banking: Raul Salinas, Citibank and Alleged Money Laundering* (GAO/OSI-99-1) (Washington, DC:, 1999), 12.

Why would large, profitable financial institutions, that presumably depend on their reputations to retain business, engage in transactions that are clearly illegal, with parties who are obviously members of the criminal underworld, and whose discovery could result in potentially severe sanctions? Journalist Chris Morgan Jones has offered two possible explanations.

> The first, more charitable of the two, holds that in each of these institutions, greedy individuals make immoral decisions in order to enrich themselves. . . . The second, more radical, and unfortunately more accurate interpretation: that there's now simply too much black business to ignore. The extent of the dark economy is so significant that banks—all of them driven by the need to grow and to please their shareholders—find it impossible not to engage with it . . . any bank competing fiercely with its rivals will find it extremely difficult to pass up the business generated by that much flowing money. For an international bank, it would be the equivalent of refusing to work with an economy the size of Spain or Australia.[50]

This view is consistent with the factors for increased financial crime discussed in Chapter 1. With $1.6 trillion in illicit money moving around the world it would be difficult for any financial institution to resist this market.[51]

There may also be a direct connection between money laundering and financial crises. In 2009, the head of the United Nations Office on Drugs

---

[50] Chris Morgan Jones, "Why Banks Launder Cash," *The Daily Beast*, March 3, 2013, www.thedailybeast.com/articles/2013/03/02/why-do-big-banks-launder-money.html.

[51] As part of its 2001 report on correspondent banking and money laundering, the Senate Permanent Subcommittee on Investigations examined due diligence practices at 20 U.S. banks, including J.P Morgan and Bank of America, that had opened offshore accounts. The committee's chair, Senator Carl Levin, concluded: "Virtually every U.S. bank we examined had opened accounts for offshore banks or banks in suspicious jurisdictions, yet few were paying attention or taking steps needed to make sure these banks weren't misusing their accounts. . . . The result of these due diligence failures has made the U.S. banking system a conduit for criminal proceeds and money laundering." "Wells Fargo Skirts Money-Laundering Charges as Clients Probed," *Bloomberg News*, December 23, 2003, www.bloomberg.com/apps/news?pid=newsarchive&sid=axnIyNZ5tqmM.

and Crime, Antonio Maria Costa, said in an interview that "the proceeds of organised crime were 'the only liquid investment capital' available to some banks on the brink of collapse last year. . . . Inter-bank loans were funded by money that originated from the drugs trade and other illegal activities. . . . There were signs that some banks were rescued that way."[52] Support for this theory is found in the fact that during the period that it was accepting dirty money from drug cartels Wachovia's profits were declining because of its exposure to the subprime mortgage meltdown. By 2008 the bank reported losses of $26 billion in subprime mortgage losses.[53] It is not too difficult to speculate that Wachovia's executives turned a blind eye to some of their more disreputable clients as long as they were generating profits.

Financial institutions may also be drawn to criminal clients because of the favorable risk-reward equation they present. In an analysis of the Colombian cocaine industry economists Daniel Mejia and Alejandro Gaviria have estimated that only 2.6% of the profits from that industry stayed in Colombia, while a staggering 97% went to criminals and money launderers outside the country. Yet, enforcement efforts remain focused on actors in the producer nations. "The whole system operated by authorities in the consuming nations is based around going after the small guy, the weakest link in the chain, and never the big business or financial systems where the big money is."[54] The very light sanctions imposed in the Wachovia and HSBC cases, where the evidence of culpability by the banks and their employees was overwhelming, supports this view of a system that disproportionately focuses on "the small guy" and tends to ignore the role of large financial institutions that are central to these illegal operations.

[52] Rajeev Sayal, "Drug Money Saved Banks in Global Crisis, Claims UN Advisor," *The Observer*, December 12, 2009.
[53] Smith, "Banks Financing . . . ."
[54] Vulliamy, "Western Banks Reaping Billions. . . ."

TRADING WITH THE ENEMY

In 1926, Thomas Lamont, the influential partner at the investment bank JP Morgan and the "most powerful man on Wall Street," announced that he had negotiated a $100 million loan to the Italian government, headed by fascist dictator Benito Mussolini. Lamont was a staunch supporter of the regime, referring to himself as a "missionary" for Mussolini. He had written that news reports of brutal attacks on Mussolini's opponents were "exaggerated" and, in public speeches he "extolled Italy's record in lowering inflation, stopping strikes, and reducing unemployment."[1] The loan was vigorously criticized in Congress with Representative Henry Rainey referring to Mussolini as a "murderous dictator," but Lamont proceeded undeterred.[2] In 1940, Mussolini formally aligned his country with Nazi Germany and declared war on France and Britain, a decision that would eventually force the United States into a military conflict with Italy.

The Morgan loan to Italy violated no laws as the United States was not at war with Italy at the time. But it does reveal the amoral quality of many financial institutions and their willingness to do business with individuals and institutions that many regard as reprehensible. As we saw in Chapter 4, it is unlikely that those who orchestrate these transactions are unaware of their clients' reputations for corruption and their tendency to use violence to achieve their goals. Rather, they display the ability to separate the moral aspects of their clients' actions from their economic performance

---

[1] Ron Chernow, *The House of Morgan* (New York: Grove/Atlantic. 2010), 282.
[2] *Ibid.*

and their potential to become good business partners. In this chapter we will see how this tendency to suspend moral judgments about clients and to focus solely on their financial interests, even when doing so constitutes a crime, is common today at some of the world's largest and most reputable financial institutions.

The issues raised by these practices go beyond concerns about financial crime. An important aspect of contemporary geopolitics is the ability of countries to affect change in rogue nations through the imposition of economic sanctions that restrict trade with the offending country by cutting off vital sources of capital. One of the best examples is South Africa where economic sanctions imposed by the United States and other countries in the 1980s ultimately led to the dismantling of the oppressive apartheid system that had forced many of its citizens into a second-class status for years. The effects of economic sanctions, however, are undermined when global financial institutions violate them in order to pursue profits. Once again we can see the forces of globalization at work. International banks are truly global in their nature, expressing little loyalty to a single country and its laws and policies, while remaining fully committed to the goal of maximizing profit whatever the political and social costs, costs which are usually borne by others.

A BRIEF HISTORY

Attempts to restrict trade with those deemed to be enemies of the United States has a long history. During the War of 1812, which pitted the United States against Britain over attempts by that country to block U.S. trade with France, the United States passed the Enemy Trade Act which prohibited Americans from trading with Britain. The Act was difficult to enforce and as a result "British forces [were] kept well fed and supplied with the help of American smugglers pursuing illicit profits over patriotism."[3] In 1861, during the Civil War, the U.S. Congress passed a law that prohibited "commercial intercourse" with Confederate states.[4] The Civil War

---

[3] Peter Andreas, *Smuggler Nation* (New York: Oxford University Press, 2013), 82–83.
[4] 12 Stat. 257.

legislation was updated in 1917, during World War I, with the passage of the Trading with the Enemy Act which prohibited trade between U.S. citizens and the governments of foreign countries that have been declared to be enemies of the United States, their citizens, and their allies.[5]

By the 1930s many American and European corporations, particularly financial institutions, were operating as multinationals with subsidiaries spread all over the world. As noted previously, this meant that their allegiances to any particular country were weakening, even in wartime, as they sought profits through alliances with foreign partners. Over the last several decades allegations have emerged that claim that prominent U.S. companies and well-known individuals from business and politics engaged in commercial transactions with the Nazis just prior to and during World War II. If true, these allegations would "further undercut the neat myths about World War II—the Hollywood notion, made ever more plausible with the passage of time, of a 'good war,' a stark battle against evil."[6]

One of the American banks that reportedly worked closely with Nazi officials before and after the U.S. entry into the war was Chase National Bank, now part of JP Morgan Chase, which for many years was controlled by the Rockefeller family. Declassified documents released by the U.S. National Archives point to Chase's involvement in several programs that directly benefited the Nazi regime while increasing the bank's earnings. One of these was the *Rückwanderer* mark scheme, a program begun by German authorities in 1936 to bring much-needed U.S. dollars to Germany where they could be used to purchase raw materials and finished goods. The program focused on persons of German descent who lived in the United States but who wanted to return to Germany to be part of the "glories" of the Third Reich. The program allowed German-Americans to exchange dollars for German marks, which would be held in accounts in Germany, at favorable exchange rates with the anticipation that the marks would increase in value after Germany quickly vanquished all the European countries that stood in its way. Many of the marks used in the program came from the seized accounts of Jews who had fled the country. By

[5] Trading with the Enemy Act of 1917 Ch. 106, 40 Stat. 411 (Oct. 6, 1917).
[6] Michael Hirsch, "Dirty Business," *Newsweek*, December 14, 1998.

June 1941 when the program was shut down by Executive Order, Chase had processed over 4,500 applications for the program, providing the German government nearly $9 million, and earning Chase $500,000 in commissions.[7] The FBI under J. Edgar Hoover investigated Chase's involvement in the scheme for possible violations of the Johnson Act of 1934 and the Neutrality Act of 1939, which prohibited making loans to belligerent nations, and ultimately recommended that the bank be prosecuted. In 1944, however, the U.S. Attorney in the Southern District of New York decided against prosecution.[8]

The declassified documents found in the National Archives also implicated the patriarch of one of America's most influential families. For years rumors had circulated linking Prescott Bush, a former U.S. senator and father of President George H.W. Bush and grandfather of President George W. Bush, to German companies that helped finance the Nazi war machine. Archived files provide documentary evidence to support these claims. Much of the controversy centers on Prescott Bush's role as a director at the Union Banking Corporation (UBC) which was controlled by Fritz Thyssen, a German industrialist who strongly supported Hitler in the 1930s. At the time, Bush was a partner at the New York investment bank of Brown Brothers Harriman. According to the *Guardian* newspaper, "By the late 1930s, Brown Brothers Harriman, which claimed to be the world's largest private investment bank, and UBC had bought and shipped millions of dollars of gold, fuel, steel, coal and US treasury bonds to Germany, both feeding and financing Hitler's build-up to war."[9]

Prior to the U.S. entry into World War II in December 1941, these business activities were all perfectly legal, if ethically questionable since, among other belligerent acts, Germany had invaded Poland in 1939. But the documents from the archives reveal that UBC continued to do business with its German partners even after the United States had declared war with Germany. Following the publication of an article in the *New York*

---

[7] Richard Breitman, *U.S. Intelligence and the Nazis* (New York: Cambridge University Press, 2005), 187.

[8] *Ibid*, 188, 192.

[9] Ben Aris and Duncan Campbell, "How Bush's Grandfather Helped Hitler's Rise to Power," *The Guardian*, September 25, 2004.

Herald Tribune in July 1942 claiming that Nazis were hiding $3 million in UBC accounts (which turned out not to be true), the Alien Property Commission (APC) began an investigation of UBC and on October 20, 1942, acting under authority of the Trading with the Enemy Act, seized UBC and its assets. The APC also seized the assets of several other Brown-Bush-Thyssen entities, all with significant interests in Nazi Germany. A report produced by the Office of Alien Property Custodian in 1942 concluded that "since 1939, these (steel and mining) properties have been in possession of and have been operated by the German government and have undoubtedly been of considerable assistance to that country's war effort."[10]

In addition to the Trading with the Enemy Act, the other piece of legislation that has facilitated the efforts of the United States to impose economic sanctions on foreign countries and entities is the International Emergency Economic Powers Act (IEEPA). The law was enacted in 1977 and authorizes the President to declare that specific foreign entities represent "an unusual and extraordinary threat, which has its source in whole or substantial part outside the United States, to the national security, foreign policy, or economy of the United States."[11] The law gives the President the power to block transactions with those foreign entities as well as to seize their assets in the United States. The law was first applied by President Jimmy Carter to freeze Iranian assets in the United States during the Iranian hostage crisis of 1979.

The IEEPA is administered by the OFAC. Operating out of the Department of Treasury, OFAC seeks "to prohibit U.S. persons and entities from engaging in trade or financial transactions with terrorists, persons engaged in activities related to the proliferation of weapons of mass destruction, international narcotics traffickers, and rogue jurisdictions."[12] Specifically, OFAC rules prohibit financial institutions from engaging in transactions "with the governments of, or individuals associated

---

[10] *Ibid.*

[11] Act of December 28, 1977, Pub. L. No. 95–223, tit. 11, 91 Stat. 1625, 1626–1629 (codified at 50 U.S.C. §§ 1701–1706 (Supp. IV 1980)).

[12] Senate Comm. on Homeland Security and Governmental Affairs, Permanent Subcomm. on Investigations, *U.S. Vulnerabilities to Money Laundering, Drugs, and Terrorist Financing: HSBC Case History*, S. Rep. (2002), 114.

with, foreign countries against which federal law imposes economic sanctions."[13] OFAC maintains a list of prohibited countries, entities, and individuals. The countries that have appeared on the list include Iran, Iraq, Burma (Myanmar), Sudan, North Korea, Syria, Cuba, Somalia, and Libya. Many of the countries on the list are there because of persistent human rights abuses or because they are sponsors of terrorism or because of their efforts to develop nuclear weapons. Violations of these rules can lead to criminal prosecution by the U.S. Department of Justice as well as to civil actions.

In recent years OFAC has focused its attention on financial institutions that do business with banned countries and entities. While some of those charged with OFAC violations were relatively obscure banks, many were among the largest financial institutions in the world. The data in Table 5.1 illustrate this fact. Between 2005 and 2014 four of the ten largest banks in the world were charged with doing business with prohibited countries or entities. And nine of the top twenty were charged. The penalties imposed on these financial institutions were large, ranging from $8.5 million to nearly $1 billion, evidence that these were not minor, clerical errors but consisted largely of repeated prohibited transactions involving millions of dollars.

EVADING THE RULES

Financial institutions, including foreign banks that do business in the United States, are required to screen their customers to determine if they are on the OFAC list of prohibited entities, including individuals. A separate list of Specially Designated Nationals (SDNs) includes names of individuals, and their businesses, who are prohibited because of affiliations with terrorist or international criminal organizations. If banks determine that transactions involve persons or governments on the lists, they are required to notify OFAC and the transactions may be blocked.

That is how things are supposed to work. But many financial institutions chafe at the idea of restrictions on who they do business with, particularly when those deals represent lucrative revenue streams. To

---

[13] Office of Foreign Asset Control, *OFAC Policy and Procedure Manual* (2011), 20.

TABLE 5.1 BANKS SANCTIONED FOR OFAC VIOLATIONS,
BY SIZE OF INSTITUTION.

Institution	Year of Action	Penalty	Rank (Total Assets)	Headquarters
HSBC	2012	375,000,000	2	U.K.
BNP Paribas	2014	963,619,900	4	France
Bank of Tokyo-Mitsubishi	2012	8,571,634	5	Japan
J.P. Morgan Chase	2011	88,300,000	6	U.S.
Barclays	2010	176,000,000	11	U.K.
Bank of America	2014	16,562,700	12	U.S.
Royal Bank of Scotland	2013	33,122,307	17	U.K.
Wells Fargo Bank	2005	42,833,000	20	U.S.
Lloyds Banking Group	2009	217,000,000	22	U.K.
ING Bank	2012	619,000,000	26	Netherlands
Credit Suisse	2009	536,000,000	28	Switzerland
Commerzbank	2015	258,660,796	40	Germany
Standard Chartered	2012	132,000,000	44	U.K.
Australia and New Zealand Banking Group	2009	5,750.000	47	Australia
ABN Amro	2010	500,000,000	53	Netherlands

Sources: Office of Foreign Asset Control. "Civil Penalties and Enforcement Information."
www.treasury.gov/resource-center/sanctions/CivPen/Pages/civpen-index2.aspx; Banks
around the World. "Top 100 banks in the World." www.relbanks.com/worlds-top-banks/
assets-2013.

circumvent these restrictions bank employees have devised elaborate strategies to hide the identities of their clients, and, as we shall see, they have usually done so with the full knowledge and approval of their superiors. The larger goal of these strategies was to allow the banks to have their cake and eat it too; to continue doing business within the United States and to continue to reap profits through transactions with banned entities.

A relatively simple example of how OFAC violations may occur involved a non-bank financial institution, PayPal. The company is a money services business that, according to its web site, "helps people and businesses accept and make payments in more than 100 different currencies and withdraw money from their PayPal accounts to their bank accounts in 57 different currencies."[14] In 2015, PayPal agreed to pay a penalty of over $7 million for OFAC violations that included 136 transactions over a three-year period to a Turkish national named Kursad Zafer Cire. Mr. Cire was placed on the OFAC SDN list in 2009 because of his affiliation with A.Q. Khan, the infamous Pakistani scientist who sold his expertise in nuclear weapons technology to Iran, North Korea, and Libya. Like other financial institutions PayPal used special software to scan its clients for matches to the SDN list. The software identified Mr. Cire as a possible match on six different occasions but no report was made to OFAC. Only after the seventh match were the authorities notified. In announcing the settlement OFAC concluded that "PayPal's management demonstrated reckless disregard for U.S. economic sanctions . . . [and] provided economic benefit to Cire. . . ."[15] Many of the banks cited for OFAC violations engaged in similar conduct by clearing transactions for prohibited entities.

HSBC

Not surprisingly, one of the banks discovered to have routinely and systematically violated OFAC rules over the years was HSBC. The Senate Permanent Subcommittee on Investigations turned up evidence that

[14] www.paypal-media.com/about (May 7, 2015).
[15] Office of Foreign Asset Control, "Enforcement Information for March 25, 2015," www .treasury.gov/resource-center/sanctions/CivPen/Documents/20150325_paypal.pdf.

HSBC executives were aware that the bank was engaging in Iranian transactions, despite long-standing prohibitions, as early as 2000 but did little
to stop the practice. As in its money-laundering cases, the OFAC Iranian
violations were largely committed by HSBC affiliates: HSBC Europe
(HBEU) and HSBC Middle East (HBME). For years employees in these
two subsidiaries had processed transactions involving Iranian clients, getting them past OFAC screening filters by carefully deleting any references
to Iran in submitted documents. These employees were not acting on their
own but were following directives from their superiors. Despite a ban on
transactions with Iran that was implemented in 1979, in 2001 an HSBC
executive told senior managers that he was looking to "significantly grow
our presence in Iran."[16] HBME analysts estimated that processing 700
Iranian transactions a day would bring in $4 million in income a year.[17]

Internal documents confirm the fact that evading OFAC rules in order
to do business with Iranian clients was established policy at HSBC affiliates. In 2001, for example, a manager in the HSBC office in London in-
structed a manager at the London office of Bank Melli, Iran's largest bank
which is run by the Iranian government, on how to complete documents
so as not to raise OFAC red flags. The discussion focused on how to fill in
a certain section (field 52) in the form sent to OFAC that lists the party
with whom a transaction is being conducted; the goal was to prevent any
mention of the Iranian bank, which might trigger an OFAC review.

> The key is to **always** populate **field 52**—if you do not have
> an ordering party name then quote "One of our Clients",
> **never leave blank**. This means that the outgoing payment
> instruction from HSBC will not quote Bank Melli as sender—
> just HSBC and whatever is in field 52.[18]

In 2004, after an HBME executive had threatened to cease all business with
Iranian banks, another executive responded by saying that if that were to

[16] Permanent Subcommittee, *U.S. Vulnerabilities*, 119.
[17] *Ibid.*
[18] *Ibid.*, 123–124 (emphasis in the original).

happen, "we will effectively be insulting the Government and the State of Iran . . . [and] to exit business which we have been conducting for many years would jeopardize all other existing business activities."[19] The latter point is buttressed by the fact that between 2001 and 2007, HSBC affiliates processed an estimated 25,000 transactions involving Iran totaling $19.4 billion.[20]

Iran was not the only banned country with which HSBC did business. The bank also processed transactions for customers in Sudan, Cuba, Burma, and North Korea. The Subcommittee also learned that correspondent accounts, denominated in U.S. dollars, had been established in the U.K. in the name of the "Taliban." The Subcommittee took a dim view of this fact noting that "The fact that HBEU had this account after the 9–11 terrorist attack on the United States again demonstrates how HSBC affiliates took on high risk accounts that exposed the U.S. financial system to money laundering and terrorist financing risks."[21]

BNP Paribas

One of the largest penalties imposed on a bank for OFAC violations was the nearly $9 billion that French bank, BNP Paribas (BNPP) agreed to pay to settle charges that from 2004 through 2012 it had "willfully move[d] at least $8,833,600,000 through the U.S financial system on behalf of Sanctioned Entities in violation of U.S. sanctions laws. . . ."[22] With 190,000 employees and 34 million customers worldwide BNPP is the largest bank in France and one of the five largest banks in the world.[23] The bank has affiliates and subsidiaries around the globe, including offices in New York, where it has a significant presence. The indictment filed against BNPP focused on its dealings with the Sudan.

In 1997 President Clinton, citing "continued support for international terrorism; ongoing efforts to destabilize neighboring governments, and

---

[19] *Ibid.*, 146.

[20] *Ibid.*, 165.

[21] *Ibid.*, 176.

[22] *United States v. BNP Paribas*, Case No. 1:14-cr-00460 (SDNY 2014), ("Statement of Facts"), 5.

[23] *Ibid.*, 1.

the prevalence of human rights violations including slavery and the denial of religious freedom," issued an executive order imposing trade sanctions on this conflict-ridden African nation.[24] For decades the country has been torn apart by civil wars leading to the deaths of hundreds of thousands of its citizens and the displacement of millions more. Sudan is one of the poorest countries in the world despite being oil-rich. One of the main reasons why little of these riches reach most citizens is the country's exceptionally corrupt government, whose members routinely loot money from the public coffers for their own benefit. Transparency International has ranked Sudan 165th out of 168 countries on its global corruption scale.[25] The sanctions imposed on the country meant that "virtually all trade and investment activities involving the U.S. financial system, including the processing of U.S. dollar transactions through the United States, were prohibited."[26]

Despite these restrictions, between 2002 and 2007, BNPP's Swiss subsidiary BNPP Geneva, reportedly processed dollar-denominated transactions for Sudanese clients with a total value of $4 billion, most of which involved a bank owned by the Sudanese government. One of the methods BNPP used to evade the OFAC filters that would have blocked these transactions was to simply omit any references to Sudan in its filing documents. Internally, BNPP employees would flag these documents with clear instructions like: "! Payment in $ to [French Bank 1] without mentioning Sudan to N.Y.!!!" [27] Another method used by BNPP to disguise its Sudanese transactions was to process them through an outside or "satellite bank." Funds held by a Sudanese bank in BNPP Geneva accounts would be transferred to another account held by the satellite bank. The money would then be transferred to the intended beneficiary of the transaction through a U.S. bank with no mention of the Sudanese client. Thus, the transaction appeared to be coming from the satellite bank not from a Sudanese bank.[28] This method allowed BNPP Geneva to "process

[24] *Ibid.*
[25] Transparency International, "Corruption by Country/Territory" (2016), www.transparency.org/country/#SDN.
[26] *United States v. BNP,* 3.
[27] *Ibid.,* 9.
[28] *Ibid.,* 10.

thousands of U.S. dollar transactions, worth billions of dollars in total, for Sudanese Sanction Entities without having the transactions identified and blocked in the United States."[29]

These illicit transactions were carried out with the full knowledge and approval of senior management at BNPP. For example, in 2005 a senior BNPP officer wrote in a memo: "As I understand it, we have a number of Arab Banks (nine identified) on our books that only carry out clearing transactions for Sudanese banks in dollars.... This practice effectively means that we are circumventing the US embargo on transactions in USD by Sudan." Support for these illegal transactions continued even after an internal compliance officer warned that these practices could be viewed as a "serious breach" of U.S. law.[30]

Moreover, internal documents revealed that BNPP employees were well aware of the atrocities being committed by or supported by their Sudanese clients. During this period, the Darfur region of Sudan was experiencing one of the worst humanitarian crises in the world as Sudanese government-sponsored soldiers burned villages to the ground and systematically murdered hundreds of thousands of residents of Darfur. In 2009 the president of Sudan, Omar al Bashir, was indicted by the International Criminal Court for directing a policy of genocide against the citizens of Darfur.[31] Nonetheless, BNPP continued to pursue business opportunities with Sudanese banks and the Sudanese government. In 2006, a senior officer at BNPP's Paris subsidiary stated in a memo that "[t]he growth of revenue from oil is unlikely to help end the conflict [in Darfur], and it is probable that Sudan will remain torn up by insurrections and resulting repressive measures for a long time."[32] In 2007, an officer at BNPP Paris wrote that some of the Sudanese banks that BNPP dealt with "play a pivotal part in the support of the Sudanese government which ... has hosted Osama Bin Laden and refuses United Nations intervention in

[29] *Ibid.*

[30] *Ibid.*, 19.

[31] United Human Rights Council, "Genocide in Darfur" (March 18, 2015), www.unitedhumanrights.org/genocide/genocide-in-sudan.htm.

[32] *Ibid.*

Darfur."[33] In the same year another BNPP Paris executive warned that: "In a context where the International Community puts pressure to bring an end to bring an end to the dramatic situation in Darfur, no one would understand why BNP Paribas persists [in Sudan] which could be interpreted as supporting the leaders in place."[34]

One of the striking things that emerges from the documents cited in the *BNP Paribas* case is the level of corporate amorality present in the bank, and presumably other financial institutions. There is no evidence that the firm's employees actually agreed with the practices of the Sudanese government, but they also never raised any moral objections to supporting the brutal and completely corrupt regime by functioning as its global banker. Instead, all they seemed to see in Sudan was a lucrative business opportunity. In 2007, after the horrors of Darfur had been revealed to the world, a senior BNPP officer wrote: "For many years, the Sudan has traditionally generated a major source of business for BNPP Geneva ... relationships developed over the years with directors of Sudanese financial institutions and traditional practices have over the years led to a major source of income, which is now recurring income."[35]

Seen from a broader perspective this attitude represents what philosopher Hannah Arendt called the *banality of evil*, a thoughtless tendency to engage in horrific behavior, a willingness to go along with what others are doing, in order to be accepted by a larger organization.[36] In the corporate context, sociologist Stuart Hills referred to this condition as an "ethical numbness" and a "moral *indifference* to the consequences of corporate lawbreaking."[37] Hills states that understanding this attitude requires us to look away from the individuals involved, who may be quite decent in other respects, and toward "the culture and structure of large-scale bureaucratic

---

[33] *United States v. BNP*, "Statement of Facts," 8

[34] *Ibid.*

[35] *Ibid.*, 19.

[36] Hannah Arendt, *Eichmann in Jerusalem: A Report on the Banality of Evil* (New York: Viking Press, 1963); Hannah Arendt, *Hannah Arendt: The Last Interview* (New York: Melville House, 2013).

[37] Stuart Hills, *Corporate Violence: Injury and Death for Profit* (New York: Rowman and Littlefield, 1987), 190 (emphasis in the original).

organizations within a particular political economy."[38] Bank officers writing memos about lucrative business arrangements with government-sponsored banks in Sudan knowing full well the human atrocities being committed by that government reflects the same kind of "moral indifference" evidenced by analysts at the Ford Motor Co. in the early 1970s when they wrote up their infamous cost-benefit analysis of recalling Pinto automobiles with a fatal design flaw in which they put a dollar value on human lives and concluded it would be cheaper to pay off future victims' families than to recall the cars.[39] In both cases the individuals involved display a bureaucratically induced thoughtlessness which compels them not to consider the human consequences of their actions while at the same time providing them a *post hoc* rationale of "I was only doing my job."

Standard Chartered

In August 2012 a little-known regulatory agency, the New York State Department of Financial Services, was thrust into the media limelight when it accused a British bank, Standard Chartered (SCB), of operating as a "rogue institution" that violated U.S. laws prohibiting financial transactions with Iran. Specifically, the agency alleged that:

> For almost ten years, SCB schemed with the Government of Iran and hid from regulators roughly 60,000 secret transactions, involving at least $250 billion, and reaping SCB hundreds of millions of dollars in fees . . . [leaving] the U.S. financial system vulnerable to terrorists, weapons dealers, drug kingpins and corrupt regimes. . . .[40]

Standard Chartered, which has its headquarters in London, was founded over 150 years ago and has over 1,700 offices around the world. In 2011, the

[38] *Ibid.*

[39] Francis Cullen, Gray Cavendar and William Maakestad, *Corporate Crime Under Attack* (Cincinnati: Anderson, 1987).

[40] New York State Department of Financial Services, "In the Matter of Standard Chartered Bank" ("Order Pursuant to Banking Law § 39"), 1.

firm reported $17.6 billion in income and $5 billion in profits.[41] A significant part of its business came from its U.S. dollar clearing operation which was clearing $190 million a day for its clients.[42] The company's web site describes its core values in the following way: "Everything we do is about being Here for good—in business, through life, and when it matters most for our clients."[43]

Standard Chartered disguised the identities of its Iranian clients in order to circumvent OFAC scrutiny by engaging in a practice known as "wire stripping" in which all references to Iran were removed from wire transfer messages. That such practices were illegal was clearly recognized by the firm's senior management, one of whom wrote in a 2006 memo:

> Firstly," we believe [the Iranian business] needs urgent reviewing at the Group level to evaluate if its returns and strategic benefits are . . . still commensurate with the potential to cause very serious or even catastrophic reputational damage to the Group . . . "[s]econdly, there is equally importantly potential of risk of subjecting management in US and London (e.g. you and I) and elsewhere to personal reputational damages and/or serious criminal liability.[44]

Despite these concerns, the bank continued its lucrative dollar-clearing business for Iranian clients, even creating a manual for employees which provided "step-by-step wire stripping instructions."

Some of SCB's senior executives took a defiant view of U.S. regulations, seeing them as a hindrance to the free flow of capital and their profits. This view was clearly expressed by one executive who stated: "You f---ing Americans. Who are you to tell us, the rest of the world, that we're not going to deal with Iranians."[45] Here we see the clash between capital and political goals vividly articulated.

---

[41] *Ibid.*, 5–6.

[42] *Ibid.*, 6.

[43] Standard Chartered, www.sc.com/en/about-us/our-brand-and-values/.

[44] New York State Department of Financial Services, "In the Matter of Standard Chartered Bank," 5.

[45] *Ibid.*, 5.

As we saw in previous chapters, SCB was aided and abetted by a well-known accounting firm in its efforts to cover up its prohibited transactions. In 2004, after bank regulators began to suspect money laundering at the bank, SCB agreed to hire an "independent" auditor to review its transactions and report the results to regulators. It hired Deloitte Touche, which soon discovered potential OFAC violations but decided to comply with an SCB request and submitted a "watered down" version of the report which excluded any reference to illegal practices at the bank. Deloitte Touche's complicity in hiding the truth was later discovered by banking regulators and the Big-Four accounting firm agreed to pay New York state $10 million as a penalty for its role in the cover-up. To be fair, Deloitte is not the only large accounting firm that has been accused by New York regulators of covering up OFAC violations for a banking client. One year after the Deloitte action, another Big-Four accounting firm, Pricewater-houseCoopers (PwC), was forced to pay New York regulators $25 million to settle accusations that it had engaged in a cover-up scheme for a client, The Bank of Tokyo-Mitsubishi UFJ. The bank had been caught doing business with clients in Iran, Sudan, and Myanmar and tried to cover it up by persuading the accounting firm to submit a highly selective report. It failed to mention some of the bank's policies for deleting references to banned countries from its transaction documents. The bank was fined $250 million, but that penalty was based on the faulty PwC report which may have downplayed the extent of illicit transactions.[46]

The remarkable aspect of the case is that the federal banking regulatory agencies bitterly attacked the New York state regulators for pursuing one of the largest, longest-running, and most dangerous crimes ever committed by a major bank.

Bringing OFAC Violations Home

In their actions against OFAC violators, prosecutors and regulators tend to use neutral, bland legal terms to describe these offenses, terms that refer

---

[46] Ben Protess and Jessica Silver-Greenberg, "Prosecutors Suspect Repeat Offenders on Wall Street," *New York Times*, October 29, 2014.

to violations of laws but that do not really get at why these acts are illegal in the first place, and how they harm individuals. But in a lawsuit filed in 2014 these harms were made more specific and connected to actual personal loss. The suit was filed by the families of American servicemen and servicewomen killed or wounded in Iraq, and named five international banks as defendants: HSBC, Barclays, Standard Chartered, Royal Bank of Scotland, and Credit Suisse, all of which had been accused by American regulators and prosecutors of violating economic sanctions. Unlike the allegations made by regulators, the innovative (i.e., "connecting the dots") lawsuit places the banks *squarely in the chain of events* that led to the deaths of those military personnel in specific terrorist attacks, attacks the suit alleges were committed by terrorist groups that were funded by the Iranian government, which in turn was able to generate those funds with the help of the defendant banks. The suit describes, in chilling detail, the deadly terrorist attacks and the sources of funding for the groups that carried them out. For example, it describes an attack that took place in Karbala, thirty miles south of Baghdad, on January 20, 2007, in which a group of Iraqi terrorists, dressed in U.S. military uniforms and carrying American-made weapons were able to get inside an American military base, set off explosives, and abduct four American soldiers before fleeing.

> Realizing the likelihood of escaping with their captives was low, the [terrorists] murdered the four Americans and abandoned their bodies and the vehicles near the town of Mahawil. Only one of the four abducted U.S. soldiers . . . was still alive when rescuers reached the scene. Two of the soldiers were found in the back of one of the SUVs, hand-cuffed and shot dead. A third soldier was found dead on the ground, near the abandoned vehicles. Nearby, the fourth soldier, who had also been shot in the head, bled to death on the way to the hospital.[47]

---

[47] *Freeman, et al. against HSBC Holdings, et al.,* Case No. CV14-6601 (EDNY 2014) ("Complaint), 9.

The suit also cites specific evidence that the perpetrators of the attack were known to be members of the terrorist organization Asa'ib Ahl al-Haq (AAH) and asserts that "AAH, was trained and armed by Iran's Qods Force with Hezbollah's assistance." The Qods Force is a unit within Iran's Revolutionary Guard that specializes in foreign operations. Hezbollah is a terrorist/political organization headquartered in Lebanon. The suit then quotes a briefing by a U.S. General, stating that when they captured the terrorists who masterminded the attack, they found:

> . . . [a] 22-page memorandum on a computer that detailed the planning, preparation, approval process and conduct of the operation that resulted in five of our soldiers being killed in Karbala. . . . [there] are numerous documents which detailed a number of different attacks on coalition forces, and our sense is that these records were kept so that they could be handed in to whoever it is that is financing them. And there's no question, again, that Iranian financing is taking place through the Qods force of the Iranian Republican Guards Corps.[48]

The suit states that between 2002 and 2006 "Iran sent at least $100 million to the Qods force through Bank Melli Iran and Melli Bank Plc. . ." and that, as shown in previous legal actions, the banks were actively doing business with those banks, in clear violation of U.S. law. The lawsuit on behalf of the families of slain and wounded soldiers summarizes the argument as follows:

> The Conspiracy between Iran, the Iranian banking co-conspirators, the Defendants . . . and other non-defendant Conspirators allowed Iran to transfer: (1) billions of dollars in U.S. currency through the United States in a manner designed to purposefully circumvent monitoring by U.S. regulators and law enforcement agencies; and (2) hundreds of millions of dollars to Hezbollah, the IRGC-QF [Iran's Islamic

[48] *Ibid.,* 12.

Revolutionary Guard Corps-Qods Force] and other terrorist
organizations actively engaged in murdering and maiming
U.S. servicemen and civilians in Iraq.[49]

The harm caused to victims' families is described in clear terms, as in
the case of a twenty-four-year-old soldier who was killed by an Iranian-
manufactured IED (improvised explosive device) in 2006. According to
the lawsuit the members of his family

> have experienced severe mental anguish, extreme emotional
> pain and suffering, and loss of their son's/brother's society,
> companionship, comfort, advice and counsel.[50]

The damage inflicted on the servicemen who survived the terrorist attacks is also described. One of those was a forty-one-year-old who was on
a routine reconnaissance patrol in Iraq when his vehicle was hit by an IED.
He suffered a broken leg, shrapnel in his right hand, burns to his body, and
nerve damage. Since returning home the soldier has "experienced severe
physical and mental anguish and extreme emotional pain and suffering."[51]

This is but one of several suits that attempt to show the human costs
of banks' overseas misconduct and make them liable for that misconduct.[52] By revealing the pain and suffering caused by the banks' actions
these suits contradict the offending banks' contention that these are
simply technical violations of arcane and often ambiguous laws. Rather
these legal actions seek to portray the banks as integral components of the

---

[49] *Ibid.*, 192.

[50] *Ibid.*, 32.

[51] *Ibid.*, 33.

[52] Suits have been filed in a New York federal court by a number of survivors and victims'
relatives of terrorist attacks by the militant Islamic group, Hamas, against four banks:
Arab Bank, Bank of China, NatWest, and Credit Lyonnais. The suits claim that the banks
bear some responsibility for the attacks since they helped channel funds to Hamas. Julia
Preston, "Hurt by Hamas, Americans Sue Banks in U.S," *New York Times*, April 15, 2006.
In at least one of the cases the plaintiffs prevailed. In September 2014, a Brooklyn jury
found Arab Bank liable for damages inflicted in attack and ordered the bank to compensate the victims and their families. Bernard Vaughan, "Arab Bank Liable over Hamas Attacks: U.S. Jury," *Reuters*, September 22, 2014.

financial networks that fund the terrorist groups that murder both military personnel and innocent civilians.

DISCUSSION

In this chapter we have explored a form of financial crime that doesn't receive a lot of public attention but is enormously significant for political efforts to control rogue states. As we saw, efforts to control trade with enemies or belligerent individuals and organizations have a long history and a checkered record of success. The fact that so many of the world's largest banks have in recent years been punished with very large fines for violating U.S. economic sanctions signals a larger issue. It has been noted that a significant feature of globalization is a weakening of the state and the rise of "stateless corporations,"[53] (companies that operate internationally and have no allegiance to any particular country and its laws and regulations). For the new multinational financial institutions laws like economic sanctions that prohibit trade with certain countries are simply practical obstacles to be overcome and not barriers to be respected. The email communications reveal an attitude of disrespect for the laws and their intent, an attitude best represented by the Standard Chartered executive who asserted: "You f---ing Americans. Who are you to tell us, the rest of the world, that we're not going to deal with Iranians." The executive was likely stating, in blunt terms, a view that was widely held among international bankers.

Another interesting pattern that emerges out of this review of OFAC violations is the number of sanctioned banks that are repeat offenders, having been penalized numerous times in recent years for various forms of financial crime. These were not isolated incidents in which bank employees inadvertently crossed a technical line but part of larger patterns of illicit activities in which bank managers and executives were more than willing to participate in a variety of illegal enterprises. For example, in the same legal documents that describe Commerzbank's long-term business arrangements with Iranian and Sudanese banks one finds a description

[53] Hu Yao-su, "Global or Stateless Corporations Are National Firms with International Operations," *California Management Review* 34 (1992), 107.

of the bank's involvement in the Olympus accounting scandal discussed in Chapter 3. The Senate Permanent Subcommittee's report on HSBC describes not only the bank's dealings with OFAC-banned countries but also its connections to a Saudi Arabian bank linked to a terrorist financing scheme and its role in money-laundering conspiracies involving Mexican drug cartels and Russian gangsters. Even the venerable Standard Chartered Bank revealed itself to be a recidivist; just two years after it was forced to pay $667 million in fines and penalties, the British bank agreed to pay New York regulators an additional $300 million for underestimating the extent of its dealings with Iran. Part of Standard Chartered's Deferred Prosecution Agreement (DPA) which allowed it to escape a criminal conviction, required that SCB employees not "make any public statement contradicting the acceptance by SCB" of its crimes, a seemingly minimal standard.[54] But even such a simple requirement was apparently too difficult for the bank's chief executive officer, Sir John Peace, who, in a press conference in March 2013, referred to his bank's crimes as "clerical errors," leading to an extension of the DPA.[55]

---

[54] *United States v. Standard Chartered Bank*, Case No. 1: 12-cr-00262 (D.D.C. 2012) ("Deferred Prosecution Agreement), 10.
[55] Protess and Silver-Greenberg, "Prosecutors Suspect..."

[6]

"IBGYBG"

Organizational Culture and Financial Crime

In the aftermath of the financial crisis that began in 2008, the Financial Crisis Inquiry Commission (FCIC) began sifting through the wreckage of failed institutions and spectacularly bad deals looking for causes. Of particular concern were the Wall Street firms that packaged home mortgage loans and then sold them as securities to investors, often hiding the fact that many of these loans were of very low quality, many would likely end in default, and the securities that were based on them would lose most of their value. How, they asked, could the employees at these firms assemble these products and offer them for sale *knowing* they were likely vastly overpriced? The answer, beyond the perplexed looks and confused answers of principal officers of those firms appearing at congressional hearings, was a common cultural attitude that had an acronym IBGYBG, which stood for *"I'll be gone, you'll be gone,"*[1] This had become a shorthand means of expressing a common rationalization in which employees would disclaim responsibility for what they were doing and avoid any of the consequences of their actions. In other words: *"Take what you can today, get rich, and don't worry about what happens in the future."*[2] FCIC investigators found this attitude to be prevalent not just on Wall Street but *at every level of the nonprime mortgage industry.*

IBGYBG, while offering a useful insight into the corrupt culture of banking, was never taken literally. It was not necessary to be "gone"

---

[1] Financial Crisis Inquiry Commission, *Financial Crisis Inquiry Report* (2011), 8
[2] Economist Robert Kuttner describes IBGYBG as meaning: "Let's do this deal before the rubes figure out the game, then quickly cash in and get out before it collapses." *Debtors' Prison: The Politics of Austerity vs. Possibility* (New York: Knopf-Doubleday, 2013), 25.

before the collapse and bankers did not try to leave their banks unless they were highly moral. Not a single financial leader of the frauds that drove the crisis has had to return the fraud proceeds that made him wealthy. The bank fails, the homeowner loses his home and is bankrupted, but the officers get to keep their salaries and bonuses and are never prosecuted. These facts points to the importance of the roles played by cultural attitudes and specific organizational cultures in facilitating financial crime. In previous chapters we have seen evidence of these crime facilitative attitudes ("neutralizations") cropping up in emails and other forms of communication, from traders fixing Libor (London Interbank Offered Rates) to bank executives defiantly breaking OFAC (Office of Foreign Assets Control) laws. In this chapter we take a closer look at *organizational cultures* and consider the possibility that one of the negative consequences of financialization is the spread of "normalized corruption." We begin our discussion by looking at some of the social science research on attitudes among employees of financial institutions. We then turn to a closer examination of real-life expressions of these attitudes as found in internal communications within these organizations.

GREED AND FINANCE

In a speech he gave in 2013, the head of the Federal Reserve Bank of New York, William C. Dudley, hardly a radical rabble-rouser, argued that behind the instability of large financial institutions were "deep-seated cultural and ethical failures" that included "the apparent lack of respect for law, regulation and the public trust."[3] Dudley's remarks would seem to confirm the image of financial firms, as portrayed in movies like *Wall Street*, *Boiler Room*, and the *Wolf of Wall Street*, as places where greed, deception, and aggression are rewarded and compliance with the law is seen as a weakness. But these images are anecdotal, at best. What does systematic research tell us about the culture at these institutions?

[3] William Dudley, "Ending Too Big to Fail," Remarks at the Global Economic Policy Forum, New York City, November 7, 2013.

A 2015 survey of financial services workers in the United States and the U.K. discovered troubling patterns in their ethical standards and behavior. Among the survey's findings: more than a third (34%) of those earning over $500,000 had observed "wrongdoing in the workplace"; nearly one out of five of the respondents agreed that "financial services professionals must at least sometimes engage in illegal or unethical activity to be successful"; and 25% said that they would engage in insider trading if they could make $10 million and there was no chance of being arrested. Even those executives who wanted to report financial crime in their midst might not be able to. The survey found that 25% of those professionals who earned over $500,000 a year had signed or had been asked to sign confidentiality agreements that would "prohibit reporting or unethical activities to the authorities."[4]

A study by Alain Cohn and his colleagues, addressed the more specific question of whether there is something about the culture in large banks that promotes dishonesty. In that study the researchers set up an experiment in which 128 employees of a large international bank were asked to engage in a contest in which they flipped a coin ten times and then self-reported the number of heads or tails they obtained. They were told beforehand that they could earn up to $20 for each "successful" coin flip, defined as either a heads or a tails depending on what they were told. So, participants in the study had clear incentives to cheat, to misreport the number of successful coin flips. In order to isolate the effects of banking culture, half of the subjects were "primed" with questions that reminded them of their professional identity and the other half were not. Since we know that according to the laws of probability 50% of all coin flips should have been "successful," then percentages above that level should reflect the extent of cheating. The study's results showed that bank employees who were reminded of their bank identities reported 58% of their coin flips as successful (8% more than would be expected) as compared with only 51% among those in the control group. The significant differences

---

[4] Labaton Sucharow. "The Street, the Bull and the Crisis: A Survey of the U.S. and U.K. Financial Services Industry" (2015), 3, www.labaton.com/en/about/press/Historic-Survey-of-Financial-Services-Professionals-Reveals-Widespread-Disregard-for-Ethics-Alarming-Use-of-Secrecy-Policies-to-Silence-Employees.cfm.

led the researchers to conclude that "the prevailing business culture in the banking industry favours dishonest behavior and thus has contributed to the loss of the industry's reputation."[5]

Other researchers have suggested that attitudes that are favorable toward illegal or unethical behavior can be learned even before individuals enter the workplace. Several studies have shown that exposure to economics and economics ideas can influence individuals' attitudes toward self-interest and materialism. In one of these Wang et al. examined the possibility that economics, as an academic discipline, may encourage students to accept the view that "greed is good." Economics provides an image of humans as "rational profit-maximizers," but a "critical and inherent problem in an economic approach to greed is that the push to maximize gains does not include a stopping rule . . .," an internal mechanism that tells people when they have reached the limit of consumption.[6] To test this hypothesis the researchers conducted a study asking college students about their attitudes toward greed. They found that overall, students viewed greed negatively; economics majors and non-majors who had taken three or more economics classes had much more positive views about the morality of greed than did non-majors.[7] Other studies have produced similar results, finding that in Germany, economics students were more likely to accept bribes than other students[8]; economics majors in the United States were less honest if they were exposed to ideas in a microeconomics class[9]; and economics professors gave less money to charities than

---

[5] Alain Cohn, Ernest Fehr and Michel Marichael, "Business Culture and Dishonesty in the Banking Industry," *Nature*, 516 (2014).

[6] Long Wang, Deepak Malhotra and Keith Murnighan, "Economics Education and Greed," *Academy of Management Learning and Education* 4(10) (2011): 644. Sociologist Robert Merton made a similar observation about American culture nearly 50 years ago when he wrote: "in the American Dream there is no final stopping point. The measure of 'monetary success' is conveniently indefinite and relative." Robert K. Merton, *Social Theory and Social Structure* (New York: Simon and Schuster, 1968), 190.

[7] Wang et al., "Economics Education and Greed."

[8] Bjorn Frank and Gunther Schulze, "Does Economics Make Citizens More Corrupt?" *Journal of Economic Behavior and Organization* 43 (2000), 101–113.

[9] Robert Frank, Thomas Gilovich and Dennis Regan, "Does Studying Economics Inhibit Cooperation?" *The Journal of Economic Perspectives* 7(2) (1993): 159–171.

academics from other disciplines.[10] These findings are very important because many business school professors have been trained in economics and "[t]heir influence on management and organizations is enormous and pervasive."[11]

These studies help us to understand the worldview of those in the upper echelons of business, which helps explain the illegal and unethical behavior described in previous chapters. They do not think of themselves as "criminals." It is a view that tends to see all social situations as competitive, in which, either within or outside business, one needs to look for "an angle," a competitive edge, or, in the words of mainstream economics, to "maximize one's self-interest." This very attitude was exemplified in a recent case of fare-beating in London. The offender was a regular commuter from the rural area of East Sussex. Instead of paying the fare of £21.50 he boarded the train without buying a ticket and then when he arrived in London, paid a penalty fare of £7.20 for passengers who exit the train but do not have a ticket. In November 2013 he was caught by a suspicious ticket inspector and train authorities later calculated that over the five-year period in which he had been running the scam, he had ripped off the transit system for £43,000 (about $68,000). At first, the man's identity was withheld by the authorities. But the media soon sniffed it out and it was revealed that England's biggest fare-dodger was a forty-four-year-old executive with one of the largest asset management firms in the U.K., where he was paid approximately £1,000,000 a year. His salary afforded him a lavish lifestyle that included owning two homes, valued at £1,000,000 and £2,725,000.[12]

The remarkable part of this story of the wealthy fare-beater is not that he was incredibly "cheap" but that *he was willing to risk so much for so little gain.* Once his identity was made public he was fired from his $1.6 million-a-year job and banned from working in the financial services industry, all

[10] *Ibid.*

[11] Wang et al., "Economics Education and Greed."

[12] Adam Taylor, "Banker Who Dodged $66,000 in Train Fares Banned from London's Finance Industry," *Washington Post*, December 15, 2014. Neil Sears, Stephen Wright and Claire Ellicot. "Outrage at High Flying City Asset Manager Who Became 'Biggest Fare Dodger in History,'" *Daily Mail*, August 1, 2014.

so he could shave less than $30 a day from his commuting bill. On first glance his behavior seems irrational, but it does make sense given the worldview of many of those who work in the financial services industry. A journalist for a British newspaper described the view of the inhabitants of that world in the following way:

> Just as every human action is viewed as a "transaction" from which to make a profit, so every rule is there to be gamed: everything, even a train fare, has a two-way price if you're smart enough to spot the gap. Right and wrong have little to do with it.[13]

Obviously, not everyone who works in finance shares this view, but enough do to make acts of financial crime appear "normal" and "reasonable."

It is difficult to tell if this view of the world is peculiar to those who work in finance or is common among rich people in general. Empirical studies—both observational and experimental—have found that more affluent individuals were more likely to cut off other drivers and pedestrians at four-way intersections; express attitudes favorable toward greed; and cheat in a simple game of chance involving rolling dice. The authors of these studies concluded that they provide consistent evidence that members of the upper class are more prone to unethical behavior than are lower-class individuals.[14] It may be true that the wealthy are more unethical, but many of the people who actually carried out the acts of financial crime described in this book were lower- or mid-level employees of large firms, and were likely to fall in the middle to upper-middle class. Rather than the mores of the wealthy, these individuals appeared to be adhering to the norms and values of the specific organizational cultures in which they worked. To get a better sense of what these norms and values are we need to look at how they are expressed in real life, how they are used to

---

[13] Martin Vander Weyer. "Jonathan Burrows: A World Where the Odds Rule All," *The Telegraph*, August 5, 2014.

[14] Paul Piff et al., "Higher Social Class Predicts Increased Unethical Behavior," *Proceedings of the National Academy of Sciences* 109(11) (2012): 4086–4091.

motivate and rationalize behavior in actual situations where people make choices about courses of action.

CORRUPT ORGANIZATIONAL CULTURES IN EVERYDAY LIFE

One of the limitations of research on white-collar crime is the general absence of systematic, in-depth data. Unlike studies of gang members, prison inmates, or drug users, it is nearly impossible for researchers to conduct fieldwork among corrupt financial workers. With the advent of email and other high-tech forms of communications in the workplace and the frequent appearance of these communications in trials and hearings, however, we can start to get a glimpse of these attitudes in action. In what follows we examine some of these communications for evidence of business cultures that facilitate criminogenic behavior. Looking over these communications across a number of different cases several themes emerge: (1) social Darwinism, or survival of the fittest; (2) financial crime as fun; and (3) expressions of amorality, or an indifference to moral issues.

Social Darwinism

The merger of the Darwinian theory of evolution and economic thought has a long history in the United States, most notably described by historian Richard Hofstadter in his classic work, *Social Darwinism in American Thought*.[15] The idea that economic and social progress can only be achieved through competition that winnows out the less capable has receded in popularity among academics but remains a prominent thread in American culture, particularly in the business world. Consider that the favorite book of Jeffrey Skilling, the former CEO (chief executive officer) of Enron who was eventually sentenced to twenty-four years in prison, was *The Selfish Gene*, in which biologist Richard Dawkins argues that all species, including humans, are inherently "selfish" in that they seek the

---

[15] Richard Hofstadter, *Social Darwinism in American Thought* (Boston: Beacon Press, 1955).

highest probability of survival and reproduction.[16] Skilling apparently interpreted this literally as a "survival of the fittest" argument.[17] At Enron, Skilling applied this Darwinian view in a "rank and yank" system for evaluating employees' performance, where they were regularly compared to one another, primarily on the basis of how much money they made for the company, and those who scored the lowest were fired.[18]

In the internal communications of the company we see a crude expression of this theory. For example, two Enron energy traders, Kevin and Bob, in 2000, discussed demands by the state of California that energy companies had made refunds to electricity consumers for price-gouging, referring to a hypothetical "Grandma Millie" and the recent disputed presidential election in which a confusing "butterfly ballot" in Florida may have led to an undercount of votes for the Democratic nominee, Al Gore.

> KEVIN: So the rumor's true? They're [expletive] takin' all the money back from you guys? All the money you guys stole from those poor grandmothers in California?
>
> BOB: Yeah, Grandma Millie, man. But she's the one who couldn't figure out how to [expletive] vote on the butterfly ballot.[19]

This predatory attitude toward the weaker and more vulnerable members of society was also expressed in a series of emails by Fabrice Tourre (known to his colleagues as "Fabulous Fab"), a trader and rising star at Goldman Sachs, where he specialized in mortgage-backed securities. In an email he sent to his girlfriend in 2007, Tourre facetiously wrote that on a business trip to Belgium he sold some bonds "to widows and orphans that I ran into at the airport."[20] In that same year he described his doubts about the future of the subprime market: ". . . that business is totally dead, and the poor little

[16] Richard Dawkins, *The Selfish Gene* (New York: Oxford University Press, 1976).

[17] Richard Coniff, "Animal Instincts," *The Guardian*, May 27, 2006.

[18] Bethany McLean and Peter Elkind, *The Smartest Guys in the Room* (New York: Portfolio, 2004), 63–64.

[19] Richard Oppel, "Word for Word/Energy Hogs; Enron Traders on Grandma Millie and Making Out Like Bandits," *New York Times*, June 13, 2004.

[20] Susanne Craig and John McKinnon, "Goldman's Tourre Foresaw Subprime Chaos, Emails Show," *Wall Street Journal*, April 24, 2010.

subprime borrowers will not last so long!!!"[21] At the time, Tourre was being paid approximately $2 million a year by Goldman Sachs. In another email to his girlfriend, Tourre, who received a master's degree in management science from Stanford, seemed to be satirizing a prominent economic theory of financial markets and those who work in them when he wrote

> . . . the fabulous Fab . . . standing in the middle of all these complex, highly levered, exotic trades he created without necessarily understanding all the implications of those monstruosities!!! [sic] Anyway, not feeling too guilty about this, the real purpose of my job is to make capital markets more efficient and ultimately provide the US consumer with more efficient ways to leverage and finance himself, so there is a humble, noble and ethical reason for my job ;) amazing how good I am in convincing myself !!![22]

Financial Crime as Fun

Sociologist Jack Katz has argued that many criminologists, in seeking to explain the causes of criminal behavior, have placed too much emphasis on background factors—socioeconomic, psychological, cultural—but have neglected the allure of the criminal acts themselves. For the individuals who commit violent crimes and property crimes the experience of those acts of deviance is often exciting, thrilling and simply "fun." Those who engage in less serious property crimes, such as shoplifting and vandalism, may be drawn to them for the same reason one engages in games. "Like games, shoplifting and vandalism can be tried again and again, with no more justification than it seems to be fun."[23] In the area of white-collar crime, fun would seem to be more an ancillary rather than a primary

---

[21] *Ibid.*

[22] *Wall Street and the Financial Crisis: The Role of Investment Banks, Anatomy of a Financial Collapse,* Senate Comm. on Homeland Security and Governmental Affairs, Permanent Subcomm. on Investigations, 111th Cong. (2010), 475.

[23] Jack Katz, *Seductions of Crime* (New York: Basic Books, 1988), 67.

motivation. Nonetheless, expressions of fun crop up in many of the communications of those engaged in financial crime.

That stealing other people's money through fraud and deception can be "fun" as well as lucrative is a theme that runs through convicted boiler room operator Jordan Belfort's memoir, *Wolf of Wall Street*. Belfort recounts that the Long Island offices, where his employees pitched worthless stocks to gullible victims, were also places of illicit drug consumption, casual sex, and other outrageous behaviors, including the shaving of a female employee's head in exchange for $10,000.[24] Similarly, a former account executive at a mortgage lender in southern California during the housing bubble years of the early 2000s said of her workplace: "The atmosphere was like this giant cocaine party."[25] Just down the road a twenty-year-old loan officer at the office of Ameriquest was discovering how exhilarating life at one of America's largest nonprime lenders could be. In an online confessional essay written several years after he had left the company, Christopher Jared Warren described how his manager in his former workplace "handed out crystal methamphetamine to loan officers in a bid to keep them up and at work longer hours" and how "at any given moment inside the restrooms—cocaine and meth was being snorted by my estimates more than a third of the staff, staff, and more than half the staff manipulating documents to get loans to fund and more than 75% just completely made false statements . . . regarding stated income etc. to get loans funded"[26]

Instant message conversations between energy traders discussing their trading activities in electrical energy markets in the western United States reveal that for the participants, financial crime can be fun. In a heavily jargon-laden conversation in 2006, one trader, Smith, is bragging to another trader, Gerome, about how he had manipulated prices on the ICE (Intercontinental Exchange) market for electricity at the Palo Verde ("Palo") trading location.

> SMITH: I totally f----- with the Palo market today
> SMITH: look at my deals on ice

---

[24] Jordan Belfort, *The Wolf of Wall Street* (New York: Bantam Books, 2008).

[25] Michael Hudson, *The Monster* (New York: St. Martin's Griffin, 2011), 8.

[26] Flipping Frenzy (blog), "Triduanum Financial's Christopher Warren Tells All!" www .flippingfrenzy.com/2009/02/03/triduanum-financials-christopher-warren-tells-all/.

GEROME: 250 mw [megawatts]
SMITH: was fun. need to do that more often.[27]

The fun of financial crime is also reflected in the humor that often per-
vades internal discussions about corrupt financial transactions, frequently
consisting of joking comments about profits that would be made at the expense of unsuspecting clients. For example, in an email exchange in 2007
employees at Morgan Stanley offered their suggestions about what to
name a new "toxic asset" they would sell to Chinese investors. Their cynical suggestions included "Subprime Meltdown 2007," "Nuclear Holocaust
2007-1," "Shitbag 2007-1," "Mike Tyson's Punchout," and "Hit-Man," the
nickname of one of the employees' bosses.[28] The complex instrument was
backed by $500 million in residential mortgages, $415 million of which
eventually became worthless, resulting in millions of dollars in losses to
the investors.[29] At roughly the same time traders at Swiss banking giant
UBS and other firms were discussing ways to manipulate Libor, referring to themselves as "the three muscateers," [sic] "SUPERMAN," and
"Captain Caos," [sic] and exhorting their fellow traders to engage in illicit
transactions in messages that read "BE A HERO TODAY."[30] The festive
atmosphere was enhanced by the fact that the traders were making large
personal profits in these illicit transactions: £170,000 in just nine trades.[31]
The cultural support for illicit transactions within financial institutions
was put succinctly by a vice president at Barclays responsible for Forex
(foreign exchange) sales when he wrote in a 2010 chat room entry: "if you
aint cheatin, you aint trying."[32]

[27] U.S. Federal Energy Regulatory Commission, *Barclays Bank PLC, Daniel Brin, Scott Connelly, Karen Levine, and Ryan Smith* ("Order to Show Cause and Notice of Proposed Penalty"), Docket No. IN08-8-000 (October, 31, 2012), 39.

[28] *China Development Industrial Bank v. Morgan Stanley & Co. Incorporated, et al.* ("Affirma-
tion of Jason C. Davis") (2010), Supreme Court of the State of New York, County of New
York, Index No. 650957/2010.

[29] Andrew Sorkin, "Financial Crisis Suit Suggests Bad Behavior at Morgan Stanley," *New
York Times,* January 23, 2013.

[30] Financial Services Authority (U.K.), "Final Notice to UBS AG" (December 19, 2012), 4.

[31] *Ibid.*

[32] New York State Department of Financial Services. *In the Matter of Barclays Bank, PLC*
("Consent Order"), 14.

Part of the fun of working in a financial services company is the ability to express one's creative side. An example of this emerged in a civil complaint filed by the Department of Justice against the ratings agency Standard and Poor's (S&P), accusing the firm of downplaying the risks of subprime mortgage-backed securities in order to obtain future business from their issuers. As evidence of the fact that S&P employees were aware of this deceptive practice, the complaint cites one analyst who went so far as to set his cynicism about the ratings process to music. In March 2007, as the subprime market was beginning to crash, the analyst sent an email to a colleague in which he referred to a subprime mortgage lender, Fremont, that eventually declared bankruptcy:

> *With apologies to David Byrne . . . here's my version of "Burning Down the House"*
> *Watch out*
> *Housing market went softer*
> *Cooling down*
> *Strong market is now much weaker*
> *Subprime is boi-ling o-ver*
> *Bringing down the house*
> *Hold tight*
> *CDO biz has a bother*
> *Hold tight*
> *Leveraged CDOs they were after*
> *Going—all the way down, with*
> *Subprime mortgages*
> *Own it*
> *Hey you need a downgrade now*
> *Free-mont*
> *Huge delinquencies hit it now*
> *Two-thousand-and-six-vintage*
> *Bringing down the house.*

Apparently not satisfied with simply being a lyricist, two days later the analyst circulated an email "attaching a video of him 'singing and dancing' the first verse of the song in S&P offices, before an audience of laughing S&P coworkers."[33]

Moral Indifference

In Chapter 5 we alluded to the moral indifference with which many financial workers approach transactions that have serious negative consequences not only for investors but for the general public. At a psychological level this indifference is facilitated by the distance between themselves and the victims of their crimes, a gap in which they *are not required to confront their victims* or to witness the actual individual harms caused by their actions.[34] This social distance also allows the offenders to feel no guilt or express any remorse about their victims who they frequently refer to as "sophisticated investors who should have known better" or who they consider the victims of their own greed or stupidity.

Again, we can turn to Enron energy traders for a good example of moral indifference by financial workers. In this excerpt from a transcript of an audiotape, two traders, referred to as Person 1 and Person 2, are cheerfully discussing the impact that a wildfire in California will have on the costs of electricity in the state and the profits that will be made on their trades.

PERSON 2:   The magical word of the day is "Burn, Baby, Burn"---- [35]
PERSON 1:   What's happening?
PERSON 2:   There's a fire under the core line it's been de-rated from 45 to 2,100.
PERSON 1:   Really?
PERSON 2:   Yup. ----
TOGETHER: Burn, baby, burn.
PERSON 1:   That's a beautiful saying.[36]

[33] *United States v. McGraw-Hill Cos.*, Case No. CV13-00779 (C.D. Cal. 2013) ("Complaint"), 73–74.

[34] Daniel Luedtke, "Progression in the Age of Recession," *Brooklyn Journal of Corporate, Financial & Commercial Law* 9(1) (2014): 324–325.

[35] "Burn, Baby, Burn" was a phrase that emerged during the Watts riots in Los Angeles in 1965 to describe the fires that swept through inner-city neighborhoods during that event.

[36] Oppel, "Word for Word/Energy Hogs."

In their internal communications financial workers' often reveal a cynical view of their fraudulent activities but no moral outrage about the corrupt system that tolerates such abuses. Returning to the analysts at S&P who rated the risks associated with mortgage-backed securities, one finds many expressions of doubt about their methodologies. In a series of emails S&P analysts openly discussed the unscientific ratings model that was applied to one security, Cheyene, which ultimately went bankrupt despite receiving a very high rating, resulting in hundreds of millions of dollars in losses to investors.

> I had difficulties explaining 'HOW' we got to those numbers since **there is no science behind it**.[37]
> [F]rom looking at the numbers it is obvious that we just stuck our preverbal [sic] finger in the air.[38]
> We rate every deal. It could be structured by cows and we would rate it.
> Lord help our f---ing scam.

Finally, in a perfect summary of the IBGYBG philosophy:

> Let's hope we are all wealthy and retired by the time this house of card[s] falters.[39]

An attitude of moral indifference is often embedded in the language of executives of financial service companies, an attitude in which moral issues are obscured by seemingly neutral, objective economic reasoning in which the rational pursuit of self-interest is taken as a given. To ordinary citizens as well as policymakers who are trying to understand the conduct, and misconduct, of corporate executives, this reliance on economic language and logic may seem like an intentional attempt at obfuscation and the denial of the obvious. Consider an exchange between

[37] *Abu Dhabi Commercial Bank v. Morgan Stanley*, Case No. 1:08-cv-07508 (SDNY 2012) ("Plaintiffs Memorandum of Law"), 8 (emphasis in original).
[38] *Ibid.*, 11.
[39] *Ibid.*, 14.

Senator Carl Levin and Lloyd Blankfein, the CEO of Goldman Sachs, at a 2010 hearing on the role of investment banks in the financial crisis. To put the exchange in context, the subcommittee was examining a series of mortgage-based financial products that Goldman marketed in the mid-2000s, a time when the subprime mortgage market was beginning to deteriorate. The panel's own investigation had turned up a series of email messages in which Goldman employees made disparaging comments about these products. In one a Goldman executive referred to a mortgage-backed security, "Timberwolf," that the investment bank was selling as "one shitty deal."[40] In another, the $700 million in Fremont securities (referred to above) that Goldman was marketing are described by members of Goldman's sales force as "crap pools."[41] The committee also discovered that at the same time it was selling exotic financial products to its clients it was "shorting" those very same securities, that is, betting that they would fail or see their value decline substantially, which is what happened, resulting in huge profits for Goldman and huge losses for its clients.

SENATOR LEVIN: Now, there is such a fundamental conflict, it seems to me, when Goldman is selling securities which—particularly when its own people believe they are bad items, described in the way these emails show they are described and what your own sales people believed about them—to go out and sell these securities to people and then bet against those same securities, it seems to me, is a fundamental conflict of interest and raises a real ethical issue.
****

MR. BLANKFEIN: . . . Our clients' trust is not only important to us, it is essential to us. It is why we are as successful a firm as we are and have been for 140 years. We are one of the largest client franchises in market making in these kinds of activities we are talking about now,

[40] Permanent Subcommittee on Investigations, *Wall Street and the Financial Crisis, Exhibits,* Exhibit 105.
[41] *Ibid.,* Exhibit 173.

and our client base is a critical client base for us and they know our activities and they understand what market making is.

SENATOR LEVIN: Do you think they know that you think something is a piece of crap when you sell it to them and then bet against it? Do you think they know that?

MR. BLANKFEIN: Again, I don't know who "they" is and—
****

SENATOR LEVIN: Is there not a conflict when you sell something to somebody and then are determined to bet against that same security and you don't disclose that to the person you are selling it to? Do you see a problem?

MR. BLANKFEIN: In the context of market making, that is not a conflict. What clients are buying, or customers are buying, is they are buying an exposure. The thing we are selling to them is supposed to give them the risk they want. They are not coming to us to represent what our views are. They probably—the institutional clients we have wouldn't care what our views are.
****

SENATOR LEVIN: But there is an inherent conflict when you don't disclose to your client that this security you are buying from us has obviously a short side, but we are the people who are keeping the short on this one. We are betting against this security succeeding, and you don't think that is relevant to a client?

MR. BLANKFEIN: We live in different contexts and this is a professional—this is a market—
****

SENATOR LEVIN: This is where you are betting against the very product you are selling, and you are just not troubled by it. That is the bottom line. There is no trouble in your mind——

MR. BLANKFEIN: Senator, I am sorry. I can't endorse your characterization.

SENATOR LEVIN: It is a question, not a characterization. I am saying, you are not troubled.

MR. BLANKFEIN: I am not troubled by the fact that we market make as principal and that we are the opposite—when somebody sells, they sell to us, or when they buy, they buy from us.

SENATOR LEVIN: And you want people to trust you.

SENATOR LEVIN: I wouldn't trust you. If you came to me and wanted to sell me securities and you didn't tell me that you have a bet against that same security——[42]

Here we see Levin attempting to frame Goldman's activities in essentially moral terms—trust, honesty, fair play—whereas Blankfein wants to frame the issues in the language of economics—self-interest, risk, markets—while taking an essentially *caveat emptor* attitude toward his customers. But Blankfein's is also the perspective on the economy frequently voiced by wealthy conservatives.[43] Linguist George Lakoff describes this view, particularly as it is expressed by what he refers to as "Wall Street conservatives," as one in which:

> Free markets are moral. If everyone pursues his own profit, the profit of all will be maximized. Competition is good; it produces optimal use of resources and disciplined people, and hence serves morality.[44]

In other words, "greed is good." What at first appears to be moral indifference or callousness towards others is actually beneficial to society.[45]

---

[42] Permanent Subcommittee on Investigations, *Wall Street and the Financial Crisis*, 133–139.

[43] Blankfein's compensation as the head of Goldman Sachs in 2010 totaled $14.1 million. Goldman Sachs (2012), "Proxy Statement for 2011 Annual Meeting of Shareholders," 29. www.goldmansachs.com/s/proxy-2011-new/HTML2/goldman_sachs-proxy2011_0039.htm.

[44] George Lakoff, *Don't Think of an Elephant*, 2nd ed. (White River Junction, VT: Chelsea Green Publishing, 2014), 128–129.

[45] Mr. Blankfein elaborated on this view in a televised interview with Charlie Rose where he explained that his firm was fundamentally involved in transferring risk: ". . . this idea of transferring risk—you could call it a casino, but if it is, it's a very socially important casino." www.charlierose.com/watch/50053121.

DOING GOD'S WORK

Many financial services executives claim that their enterprises are not only moral but "divinely inspired" as well. In an interview in 2009, just three months before his grilling before the Senate committee, Lloyd Blankfein said that Goldman Sachs was part of a "virtuous cycle" of wealth creation and that as CEO of the company he was "doing God's work."[46] Similarly, in a 2001 interview following the California energy crisis, Jeffrey Skilling, the former CEO of Enron who was eventually sentenced to twenty-four years in prison, declared: "We are the good guys. We are on the side of angels."[47] In 2009, as the financial crisis worsened and the global banking industry was being pummeled in the media, Goldman Sachs sent an emissary to the venerable St. Paul's Cathedral in London to shore up the industry's image. In his speech, Lord Brian Griffiths, vice chairman of Goldman Sachs International, sought to reconcile Christianity and classical economics.

> The injunction of Jesus to love others as ourselves is a recognition of self-interest. . . . We have to tolerate the inequality as a way to achieving greater prosperity and opportunity for all.[48]

Roughly two weeks later, the CEO of Barclays went on a similar mission to the historic London church, St. Martin-in-the-Fields, where he defensively asserted: "Profit is not Satanic."[49]

Whether any of these executives actually believed their own claims is not as important as the fact that they found it necessary make to make them. In doing so they were seeking to resolve a fundamental conflict faced by modern corporations. On the one hand, flying the banner of neo-liberal economics, business leaders often disclaim any social or moral

---

[46] Andrew Sorkin, "Blankfein Says He's Just Doing 'God's Work,'" *New York Times*, November 9, 2009.

[47] PBS Frontline, Transcript of "Blackout," www.pbs.org/wgbh/pages/frontline/shows/blackout/etc/script.html.

[48] Simon Clark and Caroline Binham, "Profit 'Is Not Satanic,' Barclays CEO Varley Says," *Bloomberg.com*, November 3, 2009.

[49] *Ibid.*

responsibilities other than those required by law. In the famous words of economist Milton Friedman: "there is one and only one social responsibility of business–to use it resources and engage in activities designed to increase its profits so long as it stays within the rules of the game. . . ."[50] On the other hand, corporations must maintain legitimacy with the public in order to function. Financial services companies, in particular, are faced with widespread public skepticism about their social value. Even the chairman of Britain's Financial Services Authority, Adair Turner, publicly declared that many investment banks' activities were "socially useless."[51] Statements like those made by Blankfein and the others are overt attempts to persuade the public that, despite appearances, they are indeed part of a "virtuous cycle" that ultimately benefits everyone, not just their own extremely highly paid employees.

DISCUSSION

In this chapter we have suggested that greed, excess, lack of compassion, and illegality are sometimes woven into the daily lives of financial services employees as part of the organizational culture in which they work. The routine expressions of a tolerance for illegal and unethical behavior indicate that these acts are not viewed as extraordinary or unusual but as simply "the way things are" in that environment. This is a situation that results from a process that Ashforth and Anand refer to as the "normalization of corruption," in which corruption "become[s] embedded in organizational structures and processes, internalized by organizational members as permissible and even desirable behavior, and passed on to successive generations of members. . . ."[52] This taken-for-granted or "normal" quality of illegal behavior was revealed in a transcript of a conversation between Enron energy traders about how they were ripping off

---

[50] Milton Friedman, "The Social Responsibility of Business is to Increase its Profits," *The New York Times Magazine*, September 13, 1970.

[51] Phillip Inman, "Financial Services Authority Chairman Backs Tax on 'Socially Useless' Banks," *The Guardian*, August 27, 2009.

[52] Blake Ashforth and Vikas Anand, "The Normalization of Corruption in Organizations," *Research in Organizational Behavior* 25 (2003), 3.

consumers at the height of the California electricity crisis: "It's kinda hard to say we shouldn't do this even though it's allowed because . . . you know, I mean, that's what we do."[53]

The organizational cultures that legitimize corrupt practices do not emerge spontaneously but are usually imposed from above. Corporate executives and managers can affect the cultural environment of their subordinates by either setting examples or authorizing corrupt behavior, either explicitly or indirectly. One way that executives can set the moral tone for their subordinates is to hire individuals who they know are more than willing to break the law or flout the rules to get ahead. For example, Jeff Skilling at Enron said that he liked to hire "guys with spikes," meaning, "a singular narrow talent" for making money, even if they were "egomaniacs, social misfits, backstabbers, devotees of strip clubs. . . ."[54] Believing that "greed was the greatest motivator," Skilling would lavish money on these "guys with spikes."[55] In a very different context, a report by German regulators criticized the culture at Deutsche Bank in which traders were encouraged to manipulate Libor rates with substantial bonuses when their illegal trades brought in huge revenues. The report noted that executives at the bank discussed the "mountain of money" that two of their traders were bringing in when they decided to award them bonuses totaling €130 million.[56] One of those traders, who was later identified by the U.S. Department of Justice as a key figure in Libor manipulation at the bank, was given a 2008 bonus of $136 million.[57]

Executives and managers may also support corrupt organizational cultures by punishing or firing employees who raise ethical questions or who resist participating in illegal activities. For example, in their analysis of New Economy frauds at companies like Enron, WorldCom, and Global Crossing, Tillman and Indergaard found that "there were

---

[53] *Smartest Guys in the Room*, directed by Alex Gibney (2005, Magnolia), DVD.

[54] McLean and Elkin, *Smartest Guys*, 55.

[55] *Ibid.*

[56] Federal Financial Supervisory Authority [Germany], "Audit Report for the IBOR Special Audit by Ernst & Young Dated 13 August 2013," Attachment to: Eyk Henning, "Germany Blasts Deutsche Bank Executives Over Culture," *Wall Street Journal*, July 16, 2015.

[57] Gavin Finch, Suzi Ring and Greg Farrell, "This Is the Trader Behind Some of Deutsche Bank's Most Embarrassing Messages," *Bloomberg News*, April 23, 2015.

many . . . instances of people questioning or resisting dubious practices . . . [but] they were often bullied, threatened with marginalization, ostracism, or expulsion."[58] At WorldCom, where massive accounting frauds occurred in the early 2000s, the director of accounting once told an employee who dared to point out a large accounting discrepancy: "Show those numbers to the damn auditors and I'll throw you out the f-----g window."[59]

The concept of organizational culture helps to understand the mechanics of financial crime. It also helps us to answer the fundamental question of "why 'good' people do 'dirty work': Why is it that people who often appear to be pillars of the community . . . engage in illegality and misconduct."[60] The particular culture that develops in an organization helps to explain the motivations of those directly involved in financial crime and how those motivations can be manipulated by their superiors to meet the organization's goals. This latter point forces us to realize that culture is an abstraction and should not obscure the fact that specific individuals make decisions about engaging in illegal activities and should be held accountable for those decisions. In Chapter 7, we examine accountability and culpability for financial crime in more detail.

[58] Robert Tillman and Michael Indergaard, *Pump and Dump: The Rancid Rules of the New Economy* (New Brunswick, NJ: Rutgers University Press, 2005), 227.

[59] *Ibid.*, 230.

[60] Diane Vaughan, "The Macro-Micro Connection in White-Collar Crime Theory," in *White-Collar Crime Reconsidered*, eds. Kip Schlegel and David Weisburd (Boston: Northeastern University Press, 1992), 124.

[7]

CONCLUSION

The United States and other nations with similar systems are experiencing recurrent, intensifying financial crises. This book seeks to explain why this is happening. The short answer is that current public policies are creating powerfully criminogenic environments that produce enormous fraud epidemics in finance. But there is a critical, more subtle point. The question that must be asked is: "Why do we *not learn the right lessons* from past financial crises?" Why are we suffering *recurrent* financial crises? Further, why are these fraud epidemics and the resultant crises getting far *worse over time*?

We are not simply failing to learn the correct policies to prevent criminogenic environments in finance—as we have attempted to show in this book, we are implementing ever more criminogenic policies. It is as if we wipe out trying to drive our car at high speed through a tight turn and end up badly bruised. Our response is to go faster into the curve, and we end up with a broken leg. Our response to that is to go still faster, and we end up with three broken vertebrae. People double-down on things that fail not because they have accurately assessed the facts but because of stubbornness and ideology. The dogmatic belief that "markets" are "inherently stable and efficient" because they are "self-correcting and automatically (and promptly) exclude frauds and cartels" has become more powerful over the last thirty-five years and embraced both by Republicans and the "New Democrats" that have provided all of our presidents for more than twenty-five years.

A related question is, "Why is finance getting so large?" Finance performs a middleman function in society and the standard economic answer as to what constitutes "efficiency" in a middle-man function is "lean." Finance is the opposite. Just before both the Great Depression and our most recent crisis, the finance industry reported *40% of total corporate profits* in the United States. Finance is no longer a helpful "middle man." As we have argued here, it has become a parasite. It does not only take a massively disproportionate slice of the total economic "pie," *its frauds are shrinking that pie.* Enormous size also means enormous power for both Wall Street and the City of London. The giant banks are treated by our politicians as too big to manage, too big to fail, and too big to prosecute. Their immense size means that they can greatly influence policy issues by making enormous political contributions and hiring legions of lobbyists.

What the free market economic ideologues miss is that they are right about the issue of competition. It is indeed a harsh task master. Even if a firm survives, conventional economic doctrine is that it will earn "zero economic profits." Why would CEOs (chief executive officers) enjoy such a system? They would never have any security and they would never make a fortune. It was Adam Smith who made the two key warnings about why competition poses such a threat to the CEO, or that it is criminogenic. Smith observed that corporations should not be permitted because the CEO had an inherent conflict of interest with the shareholders and the public and would have powerful incentives to engage in fraud. Smith also observed that CEOs were so eager to escape the pain of compensation that they routinely sought to form cartels.

Even earlier than Smith, however, an Irishman explained how competition becomes perverse when business leaders cause their firms to engage in fraud. Jonathan Swift, in *Gulliver's Travels,* warned that the fraudulent "knave" would gain the advantage and drive his honest competitors out of the market. The eminent economist George Akerlof, who confirmed the dominant role of fraud in driving financial losses in the savings and loan debacle, was the first economist to confirm Swift's point. Akerlof labeled the perverse incentive created by fraud a "Gresham's dynamic" and said that it meant that bad ethics could drive good ethics from the markets if regulators and prosecutors did not remove fraudsters from the markets.

With these ideas in mind we can answer the question of why these frauds tend to be so much larger in finance and why accounting and cartels are the "weapons of choice" in financial fraud. Cartels are easier to arrange and maintain if there are fewer, enormous firms. The last thirty-five years have seen a drastic shrinkage in the number of banks in the United States and an enormous rise in the size of the largest banks and their dominance over the entire industry.

To engage in accounting fraud, it is ideal for a firm to own assets with no readily verifiable value because it is easy to massively inflate their reported value to regulators and investors. It is also ideal to have longer-term assets where the defaults will often take years to arise–and can be hidden for years by simply refinancing bad loans. Financial firms are ideal vehicles for both of these characteristics.

The third element that optimizes accounting fraud is the ability to grow very rapidly. This both maximizes the reported (fictional) profit and delays the collapse of the bank through a liquidity crisis. Financial firms are also ideal for rapid growth.

The fourth element that optimizes accounting fraud is extreme leverage–a very high ratio of debt to reported equity (capital). Financial firms, prior to both the run up to the savings and loan debacle and the most recent 2008 economic meltdown had trivial capital requirements due to the economic dogmas that directed bad policy noted previously.

The fifth element that optimizes accounting fraud is extreme executive compensation, particularly in the form of bonuses. This enhances a CEO's ability to hire, fire, and promote and produces two key advantages to financial CEOs in leading accounting frauds. First, they can shape the financial incentives to cause their staff and outside professionals to aid the fraud schemes. Note that this creates deniability for CEOs. They do not have to order people to commit frauds but just reward those who contribute the most to accounting fraud. By devising perverse incentives, CEOs are able to directly influence criminogenic environments (e.g., in appraisals, by blacklisting appraisers who refuse to inflate appraisals). This creates a Gresham's dynamic that turns a supposedly independent outside "control" (the appraiser) into a leading fraud ally.

Second, financial CEO compensation is so large and is now treated as so "normal" that the CEO can convert hundreds of millions of dollars in firm assets to their own personal benefit without being prosecuted.

Financial CEOs, therefore, have normal motives but unique means of looting "their" banks without being prosecuted–and they are able *to keep the fraud proceeds.* The key is "opportunity." Deregulation, desupervision, and *de facto* decriminalization (the three "de's") combine to produce a financial system in which the government does not regulate compensation, capital, growth, permissible assets, or the underlying fraudulent loan originations in any effective manner. Instead, we have maximized the financial CEO's ability to craft criminogenic environments. The CEO employs the seemingly legitimate bank as a "weapon"[1] to defraud, using the firm's lobbyists and political contributions to produce the three "de's." The CEOs of the world's largest banks can in fact defraud with impunity given the criminal laws and keep the fraud proceeds even if the bank fails. This is a relatively new development that is a key to understanding why the most recent fraud epidemics and cartels were far larger than anything ever seen in world history.

We know how the fraud schemes work. We know the "tells" that allow us to identify likely fraud schemes early. We know the regulatory and prosecutorial measures necessary to prevent the creation of criminogenic environments. We know that the policy reforms would make the economy more efficient, larger, more competitive, more stable, more moral, more humane, and far more equal. The issue is whether we can break through the financial and ideological powers that have shaped our policies and created a system of corrupt, crony capitalism.

After each massive crisis there is a brief spurt of reregulation, but it never addresses these key aspects of the financial environment that make it so criminogenic. Within a very few years, Wall Street's lobbyists return to ascendancy.

The truly devastating aspect added to the most recent crisis was the international regulatory "race to the bottom" engineered by the City of London and Wall Street. The Western world's largest banks threatened to move their headquarters to whichever financial center offered them the weakest regulation. The City of London (barely) "won" this race–which

---

[1] Stanton Wheeler and Mitchell Rothman, "The Organization as a Weapon in White-Collar Crime," *Michigan Law Review* 80(7) (1980): 1403–1426.

is why such an enormous share of the worst financial frauds occurred in London.

This book began with the question of why we continue to repeat various types of financial crises despite official proclamations that matters appeared to be settled with the passage of new laws designed to prevent them. These ever-larger crises have become more consequential and affect both markets and populations worldwide in the global economy. The costs are not only financial. As with much white-collar crime, the harms include many physical costs as well, in terms of lost jobs, a crumbling infrastructure, and lost tax revenue losses, resulting in much human hardship and suffering. The suffering may also take the form of serious consequences for individuals' health. A study published in the British medical journal, *The Lancet*, for example, estimated that the global financial crisis that began in 2008 resulted in an additional 260,000 deaths from cancer alone between 2008 and 2010.[2] Our treatment of the social structure of finance and how "financialization" also involves a criminogenic culture, adds a critical dimension for understanding how financial crises occur and may continue to develop absent this new understanding and adequate preventive and regulatory measures. So, to summarize, the thesis of this book is fairly straightforward. The increasing financialization of the economy, both globally and in the United States specifically, has heightened the *criminogenic tendencies* of a number of industries, particularly the financial service industries.

We have argued that the savings and loan debacle, the 2002 Enron and accounting scandals which led to a stock market meltdown, and the latest and largest mortgage crisis occurring in 2008 all have patterns directly tied to the manner in which financialization operates. Financial crises are not "natural occurrences" or simply part of the "business cycle" as some may argue but, rather, are "done to us" through misguided policy and fraud. In other words, upon closer inspection, there are a number of factors in explaining major financial crimes having to do with a general culture of dishonesty in the financial world, and empty justifications for

[2] Mahiben Maruthappu, Johnathan Watkins, Aisyah Mohd Noor, et al., "Economic Downturns, Universal Health Coverage, and Cancer Mortality in High-Income and Middle-Income Countries, 1990–2010: A Longitudinal Analysis," *The Lancet*, online May 25, 2016, doi: 10.1016/S0140-6736(16)00577-8.

keeping the status quo in the name of "economic growth" and "free markets" the latter of which does not exist in reality.

The social patterns responsible for this culture need further attention by criminologists and social scientists more generally to uncover the workings of financial fraud and society and to build more concepts and theories. Here we are talking about *major* financial fraud, and not the everyday rip-offs, more ordinary "economic crimes" (many forms of identity theft, check kiting, etc.) which may more closely resemble common criminal acts and are uncovered much more frequently and present a statistical account of criminality produced by current law enforcement actions and strategies. The book has presented this situation of organizational and elite lawbreaking with numerous case studies, and a new lens to examine them that is relevant for students, academics, and policymakers.

Financial crime is not an illusion made up by "a sensationalist media," (which is focused much more on violent, everyday crimes) and corporate criminality is not a "hoax" perpetrated by liberal politicians or some criminologists. The best information proves that it exists on a broad scale, despite the efforts of powerful groups to deflect attention from the matter, or to blame the victims of financial fraud, whether they be investors or those poor and minority individuals who bought houses under false and fraudulent pretenses in the latest subprime mortgage crisis that mushroomed into a worldwide crisis.

"Blaming the victim" of crime, and other more systemic problems and vagaries, is long-disposed of in the social sciences as a specious argument. The 1970s women's movement alone had a major impact by debunking the sexist idea, popular at the time, of "victim precipitation" in regard to rape. Moreover, social scientists, including William Ryan and many others, argued effectively against the validity of blaming the victim for various social problems many decades ago.[3] Yet the idea appears to still be alive and well today, especially in financial quarters. For example, two of the authors attended a scholarly two-day conference following the demise of Enron, and heard a respected finance professor from a major U.S. business school, openly (and honestly and seriously) proclaim that

[3] William Ryan, *Blaming the Victim* (New York: Pantheon Books, 1971).

the reason the company failed was because investors (*who were the ones actually victimized*) bought shares, allowing stock prices to rise. As a result, it grew to mammoth proportions before collapsing due to fraud by those running the firm (a classic "pump" and dump"[4]), causing massive destruction. The (false) argument not only blames the victim but is indicative of a major and common misunderstanding and "excusing" of the *actual fraud* (both Ken Lay and Jeff Skilling, who ran the corporation, *were in fact already convicted felons* at the time). If a professor at one of the leading business schools in the country made a similar comment about rape at a major scholarly conference, he would likely be censured by the university. Clearly, there is still much work to be done in understanding financial crime. The academic's fallacious argument conveniently disregards *the fact* that investors *were intentionally lied to* (so it wouldn't really matter how much financial acumen they actually had, how sophisticated they were in investing, or how much research they had done) and that they in fact *did not commit the fraud*. The argument not only deflects actual responsibility but is similar if not identical to blaming someone for going out at night with money in his pocket and getting robbed. Someone could similarly ask, "Why was he carrying any money?" The question is ridiculous.

Similarly, in the more recent and much larger 2008 financial meltdown "borrowers," typically low-income minority members, were blamed by some for the crisis. The argument was that these unscrupulous borrowers sought to "make money" in the housing market by buying homes they could not afford in order to sell them later for a profit. Their actions, the argument goes, drove up home prices, resulting in a huge housing bubble that ultimately burst, causing the ensuing financial crisis. Again, while this "explanation" is popular in conservative quarters, and in the financial world more generally, it deflects attention from the fact that it was others who sold home mortgages to those who couldn't really afford them, and who *actually made up loan application figures,* so unsuspecting buyers could qualify for them under the current law ("Liars Loans" as they became known in the mortgage industry). The loans were then packaged and sold upstream to Wall

---

[4] Robert H. Tillman and Michael J. Indergaard, *Pump and Dump: The Rancid Rules of the New Economy* (New Brunswick, NJ: Rutgers University Press, 2005).

Street. The Financial Crisis Inquiry Commission (FCIC) documented exactly how this occurred,[5] and how in most of the cases it was the *lender*, not the *borrower* who was responsible for the massive losses in the mortgage crisis. The vast majority of lower-income residents lost their homes due to fraudulent representations by loan originators who changed their supplied financial information on applications (when it was even asked for), and by a criminogenic financial culture that knowingly allowed for this to happen in order to reap huge profits. Yet are they, *as victims*, blameworthy? The argument is specious and shows the value of criminological inquiries and the collection of systematic data to move us forward regarding such issues.[6]

The rise in financial crimes and crises may be due to numerous factors, as documented in this book, including the organization of finance itself and a culture of dishonesty; not simply that "people are more dishonest" today than before. It is interesting if not politically telling, that there is a reversal of traditional liberal and conservative stances on the reasons for financial meltdowns. Liberals typically blame the system more, and conservatives the individual more, for common crimes. Harsher individual punishments are called for by conservatives in the case of common crime more generally. This pattern is reversed with major financial fraud and systemic meltdowns, with conservatives generally focusing on the system's "faulty regulations" and "big government" rather than the individuals who cleverly took advantage of the situation to commit fraud (as we argue happens time and time again in a dishonest financial culture that has grown with, and is an integral component of, *financialization*).[7]

---

[5] FCIC, *The Financial Crisis Inquiry Report: Final Report of the National Commission on the Causes of the Financial and Economic Crisis in the United States* (Washington, DC: U.S. Government Printing Office, 2011).

[6] Tomson H. Nguyen and Henry N. Pontell, "Fraud and Inequality in the Subprime Mortgage Crisis," in *Economic Crisis and Crime* (Series in Sociology of Crime, Law, and Deviance), ed. Mathieu Deflem (Bingley, UK: Jai Press/Emerald Publishing Group, 2011), 3–24; Tomson H. Nguyen and Henry N. Pontell, "Mortgage Origination Fraud and the Global Economic Crisis: A Criminological Analysis," *Criminology & Public Policy* 9(3) (August 2010): 591–612.

[7] See Franklin E. Zimring and Gordon Hawkins, "Crime Justice, and the Savings and Loan Crisis," in *Crime and Justice: A Review of Research, Vol. 18: Beyond the Law: Crime in Complex Organizations*, eds. Michael Tonry and Albert J. Reiss .(Chicago: University of Chicago Press, 1993), 247–292.

The job as we see it for criminologists and sociologists is to identify further trends and patterns that can eventually inform policy in the best ways. As we point out, the growth of the financial services industry may be complicated, but it is ultimately important and, in many ways, *completely dominates* our understanding of other pressing social problems, including inequality, jobs, housing, racism, and common crime. Kevin Phillips, the well-known writer on political and economic affairs, has argued that financialization inevitably leads to what he calls "bad money" and that,

> It's . . . "bad" to promote an overbearing financialization of America's economy and culture, lesser versions of which in both U.S. and world history have led to extremes of income and wealth polarization, a culture of money worship, and overt philosophic embrace of speculation and wide-open markets.[8]

Referring to the Enron fraud, Stephen Rosoff described what he termed "sociopathic wealth." Unlike the corporate America of the past which was characterized more by a "patient wealth" the new corporate culture aspires to a different wealth. Rosoff borrowed a term from the psychiatric lexicon used to describe persons intensely selfish, conspicuously lacking in human empathy, and dispositionally unable to delay gratification. "We entered an 'Age of "Sociopathic Wealth'–and the press hardly seemed to notice"[9] As others noted in regard to 2008 financial crisis, criminologists also remained rather indifferent as well.[10]

The *subterranean* set of values for the men and women who have the opportunities to engage in crime in the "casino economy" (both common and white-collar), values which serve to rationalize their actions rendering

[8] Kevin Phillips, *Bad Money: Reckless Finance, Failed Politics and the Global Crisis of American Capitalism* (New York: Viking, 2008), 21.

[9] Stephen M. Rosoff, "The Role of the Mass Media in the Enron Fraud: Cause or Cure?" in *International Handbook of White-Collar and Corporate Crime*, eds. Henry N. Pontell and Gilbert Geis (New York: Springer), 513–522.

[10] David Shichor, Henry N. Pontell and Gilbert Geis, "On Criminological Indifference to the Global Economic Crisis," *The Criminologist* 35(2) (March/April, 2010): 24–25.

them reasonable and legitimate, have a long history in the social sciences. The role of opportunity and rationalization in criminology and sociology, although being central in the commission of white-collar and corporate crime[11] is only sparingly applied to the financial industry. Few criminologists study elite financial and corporate lawbreaking at all, as seen by the proceedings of the annual conferences of the American Society of Criminology as well as its journals, which are absent any reasonable concentration on the matter of major white-collar crime. One of the central reasons for this is that since reliable data do not currently exist, writings cannot fulfill the current rigorous quantitative demands of the field aimed at making studies more "scientific." Thus the entire field of criminology has trivialized and ignored elite lawbreaking, including acts arising from financialization despite the fact that these literally dwarf other criminal acts in terms of both fiscal and physical losses. The estimates of white-collar crime *far outweigh* the known costs of common crime according to most experts. One recent study, for example, estimated the annual costs of corporate securities fraud alone to be $380 billion.[12] The omission of such central costs and crimes weakens the discipline in numerous ways, but especially in being able to effectively solve and prevent the most massive structural problems of society, rather than reacting to the various criminal manifestations of these larger issues, such as financialization in society. In other words, it may help people in the profession to study traditional forms of crime they can easily measure, but the concentration on such illegalities necessarily limits the potential for improving the human condition.

The best social science literature suggests that in all organizations and economic sectors, employees are exposed to alternate values through the workplace. We demonstrate that financial workers can also easily engage in fraud through their professional socialization, just like employees in any sector of society. Learning these alternate values can more easily lead

---

[11] See Michael L. Benson and Sally S Simpson, *White-Collar Crime: An Opportunity Perspective* (New York: Routledge, 2009).

[12] Alexander Dyck, Adair Morse and Luigi Zingales, "How Pervasive Is Corporate Fraud?" *Social Science Research Network*, February 22, 2013, http://papers.ssrn.com/sol3/papers.cfm?abstract_id=2222608.

to criminality. Criminologists and sociologists refer to these alternate values as "neutralization techniques" that allow for a priori rationalizations for engaging in behavior that one know is odious and obnoxious to others.[13] As we have described these deviant values can be learned through participation in the financial industry, and involve "generative worlds of white-collar crime" that result in rational choices to engage in fraud.[14]

These basic criminogenic tendencies in financial organizations are both a symptom and a cause of financial instability. They are brought on by, and can be exacerbated by, a lack of effective regulation, which, if left unchecked, can lead to recurrent financial crises that threaten the entire economy and population. It is through these processes that epidemics of white-collar crime are connected to ever larger financial crises and the disasters themselves are indicative of the *diffuse nature* of white-collar lawbreaking, where the entire society is victimized and pays the cost in one way or another. As we have shown, recurrent bid rigging, major corporate and accounting scandals, global currency manipulations by major banks, and money laundering involving major drug cartels are present in our financial system. As if this reach of white-collar crime could not be greater, bank fraud even takes place in the Vatican. "Reputational costs" to the individual or the firm for engaging in crime were apparently pushed aside (perhaps not cleverly enough, as offending individuals and companies *were caught and prosecuted,* as is the case for common criminals; that is, "*the fish that jump into the boat?*"). *Large profits* were motivating factors that superseded all other ethical, moral, and legal considerations of the organization and/or those running it. As a newspaper journalist correctly observed regarding both individual and structural elements of bank fraud: "greedy individuals make immoral decisions in order to enrich themselves . . . the second, more radical, and unfortunately more accurate interpretation: that there's now simply too much black business

---

[13] Gresham M. Sykes and David Matza, "Techniques of Neutralization: A Theory of Delinquency." *American Sociological Review* 22(6) (December 1957): 664–670.

[14] Neal Shover and Andrew Hochstetler, *Choosing White-Collar Crime* (Cambridge: Cambridge University Press, 2006).

to ignore."[15] Financial firms, like corporations in general, can be seen to fit the psychological profile of a "psychopath,"[16] in that the *primacy of profit* currently trumps other ethical and sometimes legal considerations. It's now literally a "race to the bottom" for financial institution regulation around the world, and offending companies with repeated violations are as common today as when Sutherland conducted his landmark study of white-collar crime decades ago among more traditional manufacturing companies.[17]

We have also taken issue with the idea that profit is a "moral" enterprise and that it is not "Satanic." Profit serves many admirable goals, but extreme logic would be needed to say it is "moral" in and of itself, despite the proclamations of those who are its beneficiaries. Similarly, it may not in itself be "Satanic," *but unregulated and illegal* profits might more easily be considered so. Major economic crises that are fueled by fraud and cause massive human suffering and destruction throughout the world certainly *sound "Satanic."*

The global meltdown of 2008, the largest in world history, was influenced by flawed financial policies, lawbreaking, greed, irresponsibility, and not an inconsiderable amount of concerted ignorance and outright stupidity. Large Wall Street companies and banks, whose balance sheets were saturated with securities containing subprime mortgages, collapsed, were bought by competitors, or were bailed out by the federal government with taxpayer funds.

By actively fostering deregulatory government policies, some of the most sophisticated financial institutions, despite their world-renowned

---

[15] Chris Morgan Jones, "Why Banks Launder Cash," *The Daily Beast*, March 3, 2013, www.thedailybeast.com/articles/2013/03/02/why-do-big-banks-launder-money.html.

[16] Joel Bakan, *The Corporation: The Pathological Pursuit of Profit and Power* (New York: Free Press, 2004).

[17] Edwin H. Sutherland, *White Collar Crime* (New York: Holt, Rinehart & Winston, 1949); Darrell J. Steffensmeir, "On the Causes of White-Collar Crime: An Assessment of Hirschi and Gottfredson's Claims," *Criminology* 27 (1989): 345–358; Michael L. Benson and Elizabeth Moore, "Are White-Collar and Common Criminals the Same? An Empirical and Theoretical Critique of a Recently Proposed General Theory of Crime," *Journal of Research in Crime and Delinquency* 29 (1992): 25–72; Gary E. Reed and Peter C. Yeager, "Organizational Offending and Neo-Classical Criminology: Challenging the Reach of a General Theory of Crime," *Criminology* 34 (1996): 357–382.

reputations for expertise in risk management, encouraged investment practices that were not safe at all, and that proved disastrous. There is ample evidence that CEOs, acting on the incentives ingrained in today's outrageous compensation systems, engaged in practices that vastly increased their corporations' risks in order to drive up corporate income and thereby secure enormous increases in their own salaries and bonuses before their firms collapsed.

Many centuries ago, well before the Christian era, the Scythian Anacharsis said: "*Laws are like spider webs that will catch flies, but not wasps and hornets.*" There is every indication that this ancient observation remains true today.

There are two primary reasons for this, and both have to do with what amounts to the "trivialization of fraud" in both academia and politics, which guarantees that major corporate fraud, which rarely finds its way into government databases, and, when it does, is underrepresented in terms of its scale and cost, will remain understudied, underemphasized, or completely ignored in policy discussions and recommendations. For example, in their popular self-control theory of criminal behavior, Gottfredson and Hirschi accept the trivialized definition of white-collar crime adopted by some that focuses on all persons who broke specified laws, including those who passed insufficient-fund checks and a considerable corps of unemployed women arrested for petty offenses. This allowed them to portray individuals they labeled as white-collar offenders as recidivists and perpetrators of variegated offenses. Critics found it difficult to conceive of corporate CEOs as burglars or robbers, and they noted that it was not the *absence* of self-control but its *abundance* that typically had gotten executives, professionals, and politicians to the positions they occupied.[18]

Neo-classical economic theory has dominated American policies for the last thirty years; a period that has seen a number of major financial crises. For example, major "law and economics" scholars studying corporate law assert that "*a rule against fraud is not an essential or even necessarily*

---

[18] Gilbert Geis, "On the Absence of Self-Control as the Basis for a General Theory of Crime," *Theoretical Criminology* 4(1) (2000): 35–53.

an important ingredient of securities markets."[19] Fraud should not exist because it would make markets inefficient–and neo-classical economists
know that markets are efficient because they start with the assumption
that markets are efficient.

Criminological studies of the savings and loan crisis identified a form
of fraud that challenges such conventional understandings, and which
was found to be a significant factor in the largest financial institution failures. First considered crime *by* the organization *against* the organization
itself, Calavita and Pontell[20] labeled this looting of assets by controlling
insiders as "collective embezzlement." Later, Black introduced the term
"control fraud"[21] to denote fraudulent acts by top executives who used
the organizations they led for personal gain. Control fraud has played an
integral part in recurring, widespread, and increasingly costly financial
debacles. It results from errant policies that give rise to what have been
termed "criminogenic" or crime-facilitative environments.[22] Endemic
waves of control fraud act to hyperinflate financial bubbles that inevitably
result in major financial crashes.[23]

Hyman Minsky, the economist whose academic work focused on such
matters, used the term "Ponzi phase" to characterize this growth in financial bubbles. It is a descriptive phrase, and not simply metaphorical.
Such waves of fraud are neither random nor irrational; they occur when
a criminogenic environment creates perverse incentives to act unlawfully. For example, in the last mortgage industry meltdown, the lack of
effective financial regulation and enforcement fostered by former U.S.
Federal Reserve Chairman Alan Greenspan allowed such criminogenic

---

[19] Frank Easterbrook and Daniel R. Fischel, *The Economic Structure of Corporate Law* (Cambridge, MA: Harvard University Press, 1991), p.283 (emphasis added).

[20] Kitty Calavita and Henry N. Pontell. "Heads I Win, Tails You Lose": Deregulation,
Crime, and Crisis in the Savings and Loan Industry," *Crime and Delinquency* 36 (July
1990): 309–341.

[21] William K. Black. *The Best Way to Rob a Bank Is to Own One: How Corporate Executives
and Politicians Looted the S&L Industry* (Austin: University of Texas Press, 2005).

[22] Martin L. Needleman, and Carolyn Needleman, "Organizational Crime: Two Models of
Criminogenesis," *The Sociological Quarterly* 20(4) (Autumn 1979): 517–528.

[23] Henry N. Pontell, "White-Collar Crime or Just Risky Business? The Role of Fraud in
Major Financial Debacles," *Crime, Law & Social Change* 42 (January 2005): 309–324.

environments to flourish in industries related to the origination, sale, and securitization of home loans.[24]

Neo-classical economists and those in key policy positions have *refused to acknowledge fraud* as an active element in creating, sustaining, and accelerating market bubbles. Some even refuse to acknowledge bubbles at all. In 2004, Greenspan dismissed the idea of a housing bubble. In 2005, U.S. Federal Reserve Chairman Ben Bernanke claimed that home-price increases "largely reflect strong economic fundamentals."[25] A crucial question remains upon which any hope for the prevention of major forms of financial fraud rests. Are we still at a point where those occupying prominent financial policy positions have not made the "intellectual leap" required to identify "market bubbles" as *real social phenomena*?

Nobel Prize-winning economist Paul Krugman[26] asks rhetorically, "How did economists get it so wrong?" The short answer he gives is that "economists, as a group mistook beauty, clad in impressive mathematics, for truth." He writes, "They turned a blind eye to the limitations of human rationality that often leads to bubbles and busts; to the problems of institutions that run amok; to imperfections of markets—especially financial markets—that can cause the economy's operating system to undergo sudden, unpredictable crashes; and to the dangers created when regulators don't believe in regulation"[27] As critical as this statement is, it nonetheless trivializes the issue of financial fraud. Institutions that *"run amok"* also engage in *illegal activities* that exacerbate to crisis proportions the initial problems created by *"bad economics," a deviant financial culture, and corresponding flawed financial policy.*

As seen in the mortgage meltdown, accounting techniques employed by large companies can greatly increase reported income and suppress potential losses. Econometric studies, therefore, find a strong, positive relationship between profitability (or share prices) and techniques that optimize accounting control fraud (e.g., rapid growth, high leverage,

---

[24] FCIC Final Report (2011).

[25] Paul Krugman. "How did economists get it so wrong?" *New York Times Magazine,* September 2, 2009, 36–38.

[26] *Ibid.,* 37.

[27] *Ibid.,* 37.

making "no doc" subprime loans, and qualifying non-creditworthy borrowers on the basis of initial "teaser" rates). Neo-classical economists consider these naïve econometric studies the height of sophistication and argue that they prove that regulatory concern about the accounting techniques is baseless. The trivialization of white-collar crime is evident in the fact that economic studies never consider an alternative hypothesis; that the techniques are positively associated with income because they aid accounting fraud. The influence that such studies have on policy makes it extremely difficult for government agencies to take regulatory or enforcement action against such fraud.

The severe dishonesty we report in the financial industry is certainly not unique, which does not portend well for the future. For example, in 1980, the preeminent Australian criminologist John Braithwaite published research on the largest pharmaceutical companies. He concluded that the pharmaceutical industry was the most corrupt business in the United States, arguably equaled only by defense contractors. Offenses primarily concerned the testing and safety of their products. Thirty years later, a retired pharmaceutical company executive and Braithwaite re-examined the industry. Asked in an interview what the conditions now were in the pharmaceutical industry compared to 1980, Braithwaite had a short answer: "even worse."[28]

Media evidence suggests that Braithwaite's appraisal of the pharmaceutical industry today is also likely to be an accurate assessment of conditions in the world of high finance years after the Great Economic Meltdown. A major piece of evidence is an op-ed piece in the *New York Times,* written in conjunction with the resignation of Greg Smith, a twelve-year veteran trader at the London office of Goldman Sachs, an investment bank that at one time was described in *Rolling Stone* as "a great vampire wrapped around the face of humanity"[29]

Goldman Sachs came under scrutiny only after the mortgage meltdown when it was learned that the firm had prospered by selling short on

---

[28] Russell Mokhiber, "Corporate Crime in the Pharmaceutical Industry," *Corporate Crime Reporter,* January 12, 2012, 3–4.

[29] Matt Taibbi, *Griftopia: Bubble Machines, Vampire Squids, and the Long Con That Is Breaking America* (New York: Spiegel and Grau, 2010).

collateralized debt obligations (i.e., betting that they would decrease in value, as they dramatically did) and had knowingly been hawking tainted and doomed derivatives to its "financially sophisticated" customers. Meanwhile, the company had awarded bonuses averaging $1 million each to more than 500 employees.[30]

Greg Smith, a disenchanted Goldman executive, was thirty-three years old and earned an annual salary of $500,000. He began the op-ed piece by noting that following his graduation from Stanford University he worked for ten years in the company's New York headquarters and during the previous two years had been located in London, where he headed Goldman's equity derivative business in Europe, the Middle East, and Africa. He wrote: "I can honestly say that the environment at [Goldman Sachs] is as toxic and destructive as I have ever seen it." He maintained that the basis of his conclusion was compelling evidence he'd seen that colleagues were often much more interested in lining their own pockets than doing what was best for their customers. He said co-workers "callously" talked of "ripping their clients off." He specified conduct norms that prevailed in his office if you desired to get ahead, including (a) "Execute on the firm's 'axel,' which is Goldman-speak for persuading your client to invest in stocks or other products that we are trying to get rid of because they are not seen as having a lot of potential profit; (b) 'Hunt Elephants.' In English get your clients . . . to trade whatever will bring the biggest profit to Goldman.[31]

The media highlighted Smith's allegation that he had heard the company's managing directors, persons one level above him, employ the term "Muppets" in referring to clients. The term was first innocuously used in *Sesame Street*, a popular children's program, to refer to "puppets," but in British financial circles it came to mean, as the online *Urban Dictionary* defines it, "a person who is ignorant and generally has no idea about anything." The Goldman response to Smith's critique was a boilerplate public relations performance. But the op-ed piece itself indicates the difficulties that can be involved in an endeavor such as Smith's. It was hardly

---

[30] William D. Cohan, *Money and Power: How Goldman Sachs Came to Rule the World* (New York: Doubleday, 2011).

[31] Greg Smith, "Why I am Leaving Goldman Sachs." *New York Times*, March 14 2012, A22.

revelatory that people shilling stocks and bonds often put their own interests above those with whom they are dealing. More than half a century ago, the eminent sociologist C. Wright Mills wrote of such matters: "As news of higher immoralities breaks, [people] often say, 'Well, another one got caught today' implying that the event disclosed are not odd events involving occasional characters but symptoms of widespread conditions. There is probative evidence that they are probably right."[32]

Another naysayer in contemporary financial matters was Brooksley Born, who was highlighted on the television show *Frontline*. She had finished first in her class at Stanford Law School at a time when it was rare for women to be preparing for professional careers; she was one of the only seven women in her law school class. Subsequently, she became an authority on credit derivatives and was considered by President Bill Clinton as a possible Attorney General. Instead, she was appointed Chair of the Commodity Futures Trading Commission, where she tried to regulate the credit derivative market, involving trillions of dollars, and that was operating beyond any government control. She fought a gallant but losing battle to make the derivative market transparent and to have it placed under regulatory oversight but ran into the intense opposition of very powerful men in Washington—Alan Greenspan, Robert Rubin, and Lawrence Summers, among others, who proclaimed that the economy was flourishing and her proposal would jeopardize the giddy upswing that characterized the American economy at the time. They insisted that Wall Street would self-correct rather than self-destruct. She resigned her office and was on the sidelines when Wall Street self-destructed. Asked on television what she saw in the future, she replied rather ominously:

> I think we will have continuing dangers in these markets and we will have repeats of the financial crisis. They may differ in details, but there will be significant financial downturns and disasters attached to this regulatory gap, over and over, until we learn from experience.[33]

[32] C. Wright Mills, *The Power Elite* (New York: Oxford University Press, 1956).

[33] Brooksley Born, 2012, www.pbs.org/wgbh/pages/frontline/warnig/interviews/born.html.

Major financial fraud will persist as long as the kleptocratic corporate culture remains entrenched. The corporate leadership in the New Millennium is greedier than any group since the era of the robber barons of the late nineteenth century. And even one of them, J.P. Morgan, contended then (albeit perhaps hypocritically) that the proper ratio "between the top people and the rank and file should be twenty-fold. . . . Beyond that, you create social tension."[34] One immediate way to control the kleptocratic corporate culture is to criminally prosecute and punish more executives who have broken the law. As argued in a *New York Times* editorial, relying on big fines, long sentences, or "deferred prosecutions" where companies agree to stop their illegal activities for a stipulated time period after which no criminal charges would be filed, are not effective in deterring such wrongdoing according to the best available evidence.[35] Instead, it notes that corporate executives must face the real prospect of criminal punishment in lieu of, or in addition to, civil fines. In other words, the certainty of punishment for elite offenders needs to be increased, even if this entails relatively short prison sentences for a much larger number of white-collar defendants. This doesn't deny an "enforcement pyramid" approach in which corporate infractions are met with graduated responses starting with education and ending if necessary with prosecution, but rather supports it by guaranteeing that criminal charges will eventually result. In order to accomplish this, regulatory agencies (the "cops on the beat") must have a stronger enforcement presence in the markets and industries they oversee. With all that criminologists know about the consequences of less policing of white-collar crime, some politicians and others continue to argue for the cutting of regulatory and law enforcement personnel in this particular area as well as others.

The study of elite white-collar crime including major financial fraud suffers not only from trivialization by both academics and policymakers but also to a great extent from a failure of recognition, from invisibility,

---

[34] Peter Schwartz and Kevin Kelly, "The Relentless Contrarian," *Wired*, 2003. www.wired .com/wired/archive/4.08/drucker_pr.html.

[35] Robert H. Tillman and Henry N. Pontell, "Corporate Fraud Demands Criminal Time," *New York Times*, June 29, 2016, A25.

from its status as a "nonissue."[36] Today the need remains to fundamentally shift criminological and related policy concerns from a downward focus to an upward one. The Occupy Movement which sprang from the last financial crisis sounded a populist shot across the bow against a social system that currently rewards financial perfidy. We have documented throughout this book just how costly an unregulated economic system can be that is characterized by financialization and the accompanying proliferation of fraud.

[36] Barry Goetz, Organization as Class Bias in Local Law Enforcement: Arson-for-Profit as a "Nonissue," *Law & Society Review* 31(3) (1997): 557–588.

INDEX